Rain Forests
of the
World

Volume 3
Climate and Weather–Emergent

MARSHALL CAVENDISH
NEW YORK • LONDON • TORONTO • SYDNEY

Marshall Cavendish
99 White Plains Road
Tarrytown, New York
10591-9001

Website: www.marshallcavendish.com

Consulting Editors: Rolf E. Johnson, Nathan E. Kraucunas

Contributing Authors: Theresa Greenaway, Jill Bailey, Michael Chinery, Malcolm Penny, Mike Linley, Philip Steele, Chris Oxlade, Ken Preston-Mafham, Rod Preston-Mafham, Clare Oliver

Discovery Books
   Managing Editor: Paul Humphrey
   Project Editor: Gianna Williams
   Text Editor: Valerie Weber
   Design Concept: Ian Winton
   Page Layout: Keith Williams
   Cartographer: Stefan Chabluk
   Illustrators: Jim Channell, Stuart Lafford, Christian Webb

Marshall Cavendish
   Editor: Marian Armstrong
   Editorial Director: Paul Bernabeo

(cover) Amazonian katydid in startle display

Editor's Note: Many systems of dating have been used by different cultures throughout history. *Rain Forests of the World* uses B.C.E.(Before Common Era) and C.E. (Common Era) instead of B.C. (Before Christ) and A.D. (Anno Domini, "In the Year of Our Lord") out of respect for the diversity of the world's peoples.

The publishers would like to thank the following for their permission to reproduce photographs:
115 E. & D. Hosking/Frank Lane Picture Agency, 116 Michael Fodgen/Oxford Scientific Films, 117 Gerard Lacz/FLPA, 118-119 E. Hanumantha Rao/Natural History Photographic Agency, 119 Vivek Sinha/Oxford Scientific Films, 120 Marie Read/Bruce Coleman Collection, 121 & 122 Ken Preston-Mafham/Premaphotos Wildlife, 123 Kevin Schafer/NHPA, 124 Michael Macintyre/Hutchison Library, 125 Jeff Goodman/NHPA, 126 & 127 Luiz Claudio Marigo/Bruce Colection Collection, 128 Christer Fredriksson/Bruce Coleman Collection, 129 Kevin Schafer/NHPA, 130 Daniel Heuclin/NHPA, 131 Karl Switak/NHPA, 132 Kevin Schafer/NHPA, 133 Stephen Dalton/NHPA, 134 Haroldo Palo Jr/NHPA, 136 David Hosking/FLPA, 137 K. Ghani/NHPA, 138 Peter Parks/Oxford Scientific Films, 139 & 140 Ken Preston-Mafham/Premaphotos Wildlife, 141 Kevin Schafer/NHPA, 142 Iain Green/NHPA, 143 E. Hanumantha Rao/NHPA, 144 Kevin Schafer/NHPA, 145 Andy Rouse/NHPA, 146 NASA, 147 D. Hall/FLPA, 148 M. Wendler/Oxford Scientific Films, 149 Martin Wendler/NHPA, 150 G. I. Bernard/Oxford Scientific Films, 151 Hutchison Library, 152 Norbert Wu/Oxford Scientific Films, 153 Sean Morris/Oxford Scientific Films, 154 G. I. Bernard/NHPA, 155 Alastair Shay/Oxford Scientific Films, 156 Chris Stowers/Panos Pictures, 157 Hutchison Library, 158 & 159 W. S. Clark/FLPA, 160 & 161 Daniel Heuclin/NHPA, 162 Linda Lewis/FLPA, 163 Ken Preston-Mafham/Premaphotos Wildlife, 164 Christer Fredriksson/Bruce Coleman Collection, 165 Ken Preston-Mafham/Premaphotos Wildlife, 168 Max Gibbs/Oxford Scientific Films, 169 Patrick Fagot/NHPA, 170 Michael Fogden/Oxford Scientific Films, 171 Sophy Pilkington/Oxford Scientific Films

Library of Congress Cataloging-in-Publication Data
Rain forests of the world.
       p. cm.
   Includes bibliographical references and index.
   Contents: v. 1. Africa-bioluminescence — v. 2. Biomass-clear-cutting — v. 3. Climate and weather-emergent — v. 4. Endangered species-food web — v. 5. Forest fire-iguana — v. 6. Indonesia-manatee — v. 7. Mangrove forest-orangutan — v. 8. Orchid-red panda — v. 9. Reforestation-spider — v. 10. Squirrel-Yanomami people — v. 11. Index.
     ISBN 0-7614-7254-1 (set)
     1. Rain forests — Encyclopedias.   I.. Marshall Cavendish Corporation.
   QH86 .R39 2002
   578.734—dc21
                                                        2001028460

   ISBN 0-7614-7254-1 (set)
   ISBN 0-7614-7257-6 (vol. 3)

Printed and bound in Italy

07 06 05 04 03 02   6 5 4 3 2 1

Contents

Climate and Weather   114

Climber   116

Cobra   118

Cockroach   120

Communication   121

Congo   124

Conservation   126

Constrictor   130

Courtship   132

Crocodile and Caiman   134

Crustacean   138

Decomposer   140

Deer   142

Deforestation   146

Disease   150

Dolphin   152

Dormancy   153

Dragonfly   154

Dyak People   156

Eagle   158

Ecology   162

Ecosystem   164

Eel   168

Elephant   169

Emergent   170

Glossary   172

Index   173

Inside a tropical rain forest it is always humid. The still air is heavy and damp, full of the sounds of insects and the smell of decaying plant material. Tropical rain forests grow in a band around the world, within about 25° latitude of the equator. They need warm, damp conditions to grow; a tropical rain forest needs an average annual temperature of about 77°F (25°C), never falling below 64°F (18°C). However, once they are established, they help maintain their own climate. The forest's latitude determines its temperature, but the forest produces its own dampness.

KEY FACTS

● Rain forests need rain to become established, but once these woodlands are growing, they produce much of their own rain.

● A monsoon can deliver as much as 6 in. (150 mm) of rain in four hours.

● In temperate climates coastal rain forests collect water by trapping fog from the ocean.

Rain forests have one main requirement: the absence of a regular dry season. They require more than 4 inches (100 mm) of rain every month. Where the rain forest grows in the monsoon belt—for example, in the tropical parts of southern Asia—it can receive more rainfall than that in a single day; a monsoon can deliver as much as 6 inches (150 mm) of rain in four hours. Forests in western Africa can grow where the rainfall is as little as 48 to 60 inches (1,200 to 1,500 mm) each year, though elsewhere they need a minimum of nearly 72 inches (1,800 mm) or even up to 360 inches (9,000 mm).

To withstand the constant rain, many rain forest trees bear pointed leaves that help the water drip off. Some of the water evaporates before it reaches the ground, hanging around the trees as mist. The mist among the trees swirls upward on air currents until it forms clouds above the forest. When the clouds

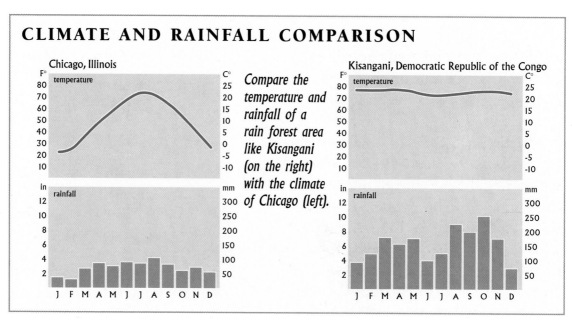

CLIMATE AND RAINFALL COMPARISON

Compare the temperature and rainfall of a rain forest area like Kisangani (on the right) with the climate of Chicago (left).

Rain pouring off a thatched roof in the Amazon rain forest. After soaking into the ground, it is sucked up by the roots of the trees.

are high enough and cool enough, they produce rain that falls on the forest, and the whole cycle starts over again.

In rain forests at least half the rainfall is generated by the circulation of water from the clouds to the trees and back again. In some places the input from outside is irregular, and the forest generates nearly all its local rainfall. In the Amazon, for example, easterly trade winds bring in rain from the Atlantic Ocean only at certain times of year. The forest traps the rain, recycling it until more comes in from the

sea. If the forest disappeared, the rain would vanish underground, and the Amazon Basin would become an area of seasonal droughts. Instead of the cool, cloudy air that hangs over the forest today, there would be a hot semidesert. The balance of wind and water would change, ultimately affecting the climate of the whole world.

Temperate rain forests, like those of Australia or the United States' Pacific Northwest, grow in cooler climates, farther from the equator, but they need a similar or even greater amount of rainfall. They also have a similar effect on the local weather conditions. Temperate rain forests trap fog drifting in from the ocean. The fog condenses on the tree branches, then drips down into the forest, where it joins in the water cycle just like rain.

Planted forests have trees of the same age and height, but old, natural forests, battered by storms and combed by fire, have trees of many different heights. As the fog swirls around trees in older forests, they present a much bigger surface for condensation, so they are better at trapping its moisture.

Check these out:
● Rain Forest ● Season ● Water

IN FOCUS

Forests and World Climate

Destroying the rain forests has an effect on global warming, especially when they are burned, and carbon dioxide is released into the air. Living forests absorb carbon dioxide, helping to reduce global warming, and release oxygen as they photosynthesize during the day.

Very little light reaches the ground in the rain forest, so plants need to get up into the sunlit canopy as quickly as they can. Climbing plants have found a way of doing this without using too much energy—they use other plants as supports. Climbers are also known as vines, lianas (lee-AH-nuhs), or bushropes. They are surprisingly strong and difficult to break.

Some climbers cling tightly to tree trunks by means of small roots that work their way into bark crevices. These climbers are most abundant in the wettest forests, where they often completely cover the trunks that they are climbing. Other climbers make their way into the canopy by clinging to other plants with hooked spines or simply by coiling around the tree trunks. Their stems are soft and pliable when young but later become hard and woody. Some of them are as thick as a person's leg.

Most woody climbers start off in clearings where trees have fallen, or along riverbanks. Light is abundant there, and the climbers sprawl over the ground and smother other plants until they find tree trunks to climb.

When the climbers reach the forest canopy, they send out leafy branches that snake their way through the treetops and link all the trees together. The branches may be 600 to 900 feet (180 to 275 m) long. Those that fail to find suitable supports simply hang down from the trees. Some reach the ground, while others may find new trunks to climb. As many as five hundred lianas may hang down in an acre of forest. Monkeys regularly scamper up and down them or leap from one to the other as they make their way through the forest. The flowers of the lianas also provide nectar for birds and

Thick, woody lianas surround this tree in the rain forest of Costa Rica. Their leaves and flowers are high up in the canopy.

116

IN FOCUS

Climbing Palms

Most palm trees have stout, straight stems topped by clusters of large leaves, but the rain forests harbor some unusual palms with ropelike stems. Up to 600 ft. (180 m) or more in length, these are among the world's longest stems, although they are not much thicker than a person's finger. They scramble all over the surrounding plants and may grow as much as 30 ft. (9 m) in a year as they strive to reach the forest canopy. The leaves are covered with sharp, curved spines that cling to other plants like grappling hooks. Climbing palms of this kind are called rattans, and their stems are used to make cane furniture. They grow mainly in Southeast Asia.

monkeys, as well as for hordes of insects. When the flowers die, the plants provide plenty of fruit.

Lianas that start life in large clearings may never actually find tree trunks to climb, but some of them still make it to the canopy. Trees that spring up among the young climbers simply carry the tangled mass of stems and branches up with them.

One group of climbing plants starts life as climbers at the bottom of trees and ends up as epiphytes perching on the topmost branches. However, these hemi-epiphytes never become very big, because as they grow upward, their lower parts die away. The whole plant thus gradually moves up the tree, a bit like a climbing animal, although the plants take a much longer time than any animal would. One of these plants needs several years to climb to the top of a tall tree.

The popular house plant known as the Swiss cheese plant is a rain forest climber.

It starts off by coiling its stems around the base of a tree, but when it reaches the canopy, the lower parts of the plant all die, and it lives as an epiphyte. It makes a good house plant because it can survive in fairly dim light.

The most aggressive vines are the stranglers. They begin their lives growing high on tree branches, but their strong, woody roots grow down along the tree's trunk, surrounding it like a cage. The host tree eventually dies and rots away.

Check these out:
- **Canop**
- **Epiphyte**
- **Palm Tree**
- **Plant**
- **Rattan**

A gibbon swings from a climber in the rain forest of Southeast Asia.

Cobra

Although cobras are found throughout Africa and Asia, only one species inhabits the tropical rain forest: the king cobra. The world's longest venomous snake, it can reach a length of 12 feet (3.7 m). It also has the extraordinary ability to raise a large portion of its body clear off the ground, so a big specimen can look a person right in the eye. It is perhaps fortunate then that the king cobra is, by nature, a shy, secretive reptile that will flee unless it is cornered.

The king cobra is quite common in the dense forests of southern Asia, from India eastward to China and south to the Malay Peninsula. In some parts of India, it lives at elevations of up to 6,600 feet (2,000 m). Active both day and night, this snake will not hesitate to slip into the water to pursue its prey or to escape predators such as mongooses, birds of prey, and humans. It also climbs well and is often found high in the trees in search of food.

Its choice of prey makes the king cobra a remarkable species, because it feeds almost exclusively on other snakes, including venomous ones. The king cobra hunts by sight and smell, "tasting" the air with its forked tongue. It stalks its prey swiftly and silently before striking. The cobra then injects a powerful venom, but it does not always wait until its prey is subdued before it starts to swallow it.

IN FOCUS

The Cobra's Hood

Perhaps the best-known feature of the cobra is its ability to rear up and spread its hood as a form of intimidation. Specially elongated ribs just behind the snake's head support the hood. The skin in this area is loose and flexible, and the scales overlap unless the hood is erect. When the scales spread out, the head looks much bigger than it really is; many cobra species have markings on their hood that look like eyes to complete the effect. It's an impressive display, and few predators will attack the snake.

A king cobra rears up in a warning display, an important survival technique that protects it from predators.

King cobras are snake–eaters. This king cobra is 12 ft. (4 m) long but can swallow a rat snake measuring 8 ft. (2.5 m).

King cobras eat large species of snakes such as pythons and highly venomous ones such as kraits (KRIETS) and other cobras. The cobra's lower jaw, like that of most snakes, can be disjointed to allow its mouth to stretch over large prey. The jaws move first to one side and then the other as they work their way down the prey's body, forcing it down into the cobra's stomach. The king cobra can even swallow snakes longer than itself by crushing them inside its stomach. Once it has swallowed a large reptile, the cobra may go days, even weeks, before it has to find another meal.

During the breeding season, the male king cobra tracks down a female by detecting her pheromones, chemicals that she emits when she is ready to mate. He wraps his body around her during mating. Once fertilized, she, unusually among snakes, constructs a nest by amassing a pile of dead leaves. At the center of this mound, she will lay her 20 to 40 white, leathery eggs. She will then remain close to the nest to protect it from potential egg thieves.

The eggs hatch some two to three months later, and the hatchlings, black with yellow stripes, measure around 18½ inches (47 cm) long. Completely independent from the time they hatch, these babies are fully equipped with venom glands and fangs. They hunt for their first meal within a week or two. They are ready to breed by the time they are five or six years old and can live to be 25 years old. The king cobra's venom is equally potent from hatchling to full size and can kill a person within fifteen minutes of injection.

Check these out:
● Reptile ● Snake

Over four thousand species of cockroach live on this planet, and a large number are found in tropical rain forests around the world. Cockroaches are oval. Many species have wings that cover their backs, and their head supports a pair of long antennae. They vary enormously, especially in size. One of the largest is the giant tropical cockroach, which can reach a length of 3 inches (8 cm). It lives on the rain forest floor in Panama and other parts of Central America. Others, such as the wood roaches, are smaller, wingless, and feed on rotting wood, burrowing through it as they go. The smallest cockroaches are less than a third of an inch (less than 1 cm) long and inhabit bromeliads (broe-MEE-lee-ads) and other epiphytic plants. Some rain forest cockroaches are brown; others are brightly colored, often as a warning to predators that they taste awful. Basically nocturnal, cockroaches run remarkably fast.

Hatchling cockroaches are miniature versions of their parents. The only exception is that winged species do not develop wings until they reach adult size. As they grow, these insects undergo a series of molts; wings appear only after the final molt.

Most species of cockroach reproduce in the same way. The eggs are laid in a packet called an ootheca (oe-uh-THEE-kuh), where there may be between six and sixty eggs. Some species simply drop the ootheca, and the eggs hatch five or six weeks later. In other species the female carries the ootheca around, gripped by the tip of her abdomen. However, a number of species retain the ootheca inside the body and give birth to live young.

The Madagscan hissing cockroach is a large, terrestrial, wingless species that bears live young.

Hissing Cockroaches

The Madagascan hissing cockroach is a giant, nearly 3 inches (8 cm) long. It inhabits the forests of Madagascar, where it forages on the forest floor in search of leaves, fruits, and seeds. This cockroach has the ability to hiss loudly when disturbed to frighten off its predators. It does this by expelling air through its spiracles, breathing holes along the sides of its body.

Check these out:

- Insect - Invertebrate - Nocturnal Animal

The tropical rain forest is a noisy place. There is a constant chorus of insects—of buzzes, zings, the metallic rasping of cicadas, and the nonstop whine of mosquitoes. As if this were not enough, many different birdcalls echo through the woods, joined by the occasional roar or howl of a large mammal in the undergrowth or high in the treetops. At night the forest is still noisy: crickets and frogs take up the chorus, along with the owls and persistent mosquitoes.

KEY FACTS

● Slave-making ants produce a scent that affects other ants so much that they are almost paralyzed "with fear" and thus easy to take captive.

● Even plants communicate by scent. If a tree is attacked by insects, it may produce scented chemicals that waft to nearby trees, causing them to produce insect-repelling chemicals in their tissues.

● Snakes hiss when threatened, and so do some caterpillars. Caterpillars also puff themselves up to display eyelike markings on their head or tail, making them look like small snakes.

Sound Signals

Why all this noise? There are four main reasons why animals make noises: to warn of danger, to frighten an attacker, to proclaim a territory, or to attract a mate. Communal animals, such as monkeys, also use sounds to express emotions, keep the group together, and coordinate hunting and food gathering.

In the deep rain forest, with its dim light and tangle of shrubs, lianas (vines), and hanging branches, sight is useful only when animals are very close to each

A male cricket (left) sings to a female by rubbing its wings together to create a chirping sound.

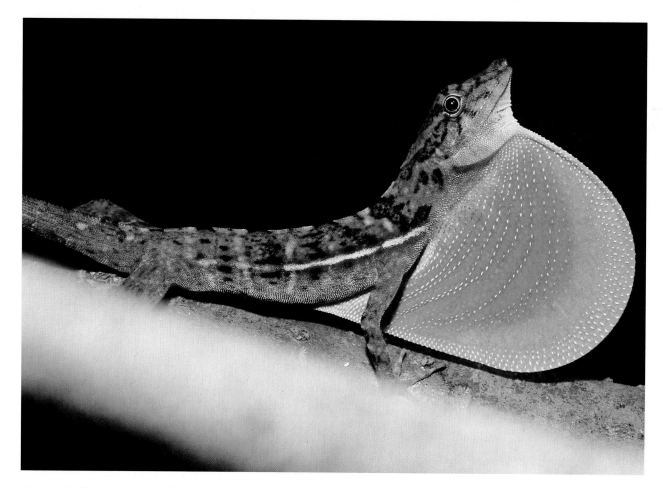

Some male lizards, such as this anole, inflate colorful throat pouches when faced with a rival or a mate.

other. Even sound does not travel far in dense vegetation. Birds of the forest floor, such as the cassowary and the argus pheasant, use low-pitched, booming sounds, as these travel better through the bush. Birds of the treetops often have higher calls. Many use a small repeated series of notes that stand out against the forest's background noise.

Birds and mammals use different calls for courtship, defending their territory, attacking, and raising the alarm. Monkey warning calls differ when the danger comes from the sky, in the form of an eagle for example, or the ground below, as in the case of a snake.

Surprisingly the loudest calls in the forest are often those of insects,

especially large-winged ones called cicadas (suh-KAE-duhs). Once they reach adulthood, male cicadas of some species have only a few days to find a mate before they die. They vibrate a kind of drum on each side of their abdomen to make the noise and detect sound through sensors on their knees. Crickets, on the other hand, use mounds on their wings to make noise, while grasshoppers rub their legs together. Earwigs use the vibrations of their pincers to detect sounds, spiders use the hairs on their legs, while mosquitoes use hairs on their antennae to distinguish the buzz of female wings in a crowd.

Body Language
Like humans, monkeys use sounds, facial expressions, and body postures to communicate, expressing affection, threats,

and "apologies," coordinating hunting tactics, and letting each other know who is boss. When a female baboon is ready to mate, part of her rump swells and turns bright pink, a clear signal to the males of the troop. Many deer have a white rump; by raising their tail and flashing their rump, they can alert other members of the herd to danger.

Who's Who?

It is important to be able to recognize other members of your own species and to distinguish between males and females if you want to find a mate, defend a territory, or avoid being attacked. Toucans have huge colorful beaks that act like flags to signal to mates or to alert other toucans to sources of food. Many monkeys and other forest mammals have identifying patches of white or other colors on their face or limbs.

Some male lizards inflate colorful throat pouches. Courting birds, fish, and even butterflies use displays of color, and special postures and dances show off colorful parts of the body to attract potential mates or to compete with rival suitors.

Scent Trails

Not all signals are obvious to humans. Scent trails large and small wind through the forest and provide a discrete language of communication. Across the forest floor and up the tree trunks and branches, ants leave trails of scent chemicals produced at the tips of their abdomens. These tell other ants the way to sources of food or the route back to the nest. They also tell rival colonies who is where.

Larger scent trails are left by mammals, which produce scent from various glands. Many cats have glands on their feet and

behind their heads for marking their territory. These scents warn off other cats and so reduce encounters between nearby territory owners, saving a lot of energy and aggression. Many tree-dwelling mammals, such as tree shrews and galagos, leave their distinctive odors on branches and twigs.

Check these out:
- Bird ● Chimpanzee ● Cicada ● Courtship
- Grasshopper, Cricket, and Katydid
- Insect ● Lizard
- Mammal ● Monkey

Howler Monkeys

Howler monkeys live in Central and South America. A male howler monkey makes an almost deafening roar. He pouts his pink lips and opens his mouth wide, and his throat swells as he roars across the treetops. His voice box contains a special bone with a hole in it. As he roars, this causes the same effect as blowing over the top of a bottle. A chorus of howler monkeys often occurs when the various troops are proclaiming their territorial rights to one another. The sound can be heard over a mile (1.6 km) away.

The Congo River, or Rio Zaire, flows through the heart of the African continent. Its course follows a great curve through the Democratic Republic of the Congo, crossing the equator and forming part of the border with the Congo Republic. The basin, or drainage area, of the Congo River is vast, covering about 1,430,000 square miles (3,700,000 km²). About 390,000 square miles (1,000,000 km²) of the Congo River basin are blanketed by a rain forest, which is the second largest in the world. Forests also extend along river valleys into nearby grassland regions. The forest climate is steamy and warm throughout the year, generally around 77°F (25°C). The average rainfall for the year is about 80 inches (2,000 mm) but decreases sharply at the northern and southern fringes.

KEY FACTS

● **The Congo River basin holds the second largest rain forest in the world, with one-fifth of the world's remaining rain forest ecosystems.**

● **More than 265 bird species live in the Congo rain forest.**

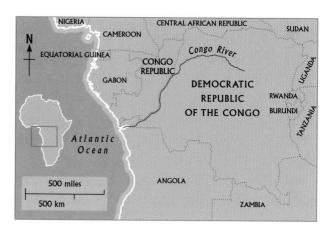

The Living Forest

The forest canopy forms a green mass nearly 100 feet (30 m) above ground level, with larger trees breaking through in places. Tall tree species include the hardwood sapele, or African mahogany, which has yellow flowers and large seedpods. At lower levels grow trees such as ebony, oil palms with their spearlike fronds, and tangles of creepers. The forest floor is littered with twigs and leaves, rotten tree stumps, and occasional flowers, such as white arum lilies or dark blue African violets.

The Congo lowland rain forest is home to many different primate species, including gorillas and

Vegetation hangs over the Congo River not far from Kinshasa, capital of the Democratic Republic of the Congo.

chimpanzees. A relative of the giraffe, the okapi (oe-KAH-pee) also lives in the forest. It has a reddish coat and white stripes on its front legs. Deadly gaboon vipers coil on the forest floor. More than 265 bird species live in the Congo rain forest, including gray parrots, hornbills, and flycatchers. It is also home to forest elephants.

Peoples of the Forest

Large areas of the forest remain uninhabited, but in remote areas small bands of hunter-gatherers live by hunting porcupines, antelope, and monkeys; by fishing; and by gathering berries, mushrooms, insect grubs, and wild honey. Some of these are exchanged for farm produce and tools in the villages. Tribes include the Mbuti, Efe, Baka, and Twa peoples. Forest peoples such as the Mbuti are slightly built and wiry. They are the shortest people in the world, with most adults between 53 and 62 inches (135 and 158 cm) tall.

Most villagers and town dwellers living in the Congo River basin are taller, the descendants of farming peoples who long ago settled along the riverbanks and cleared land for growing yams. Crops grown today include a starchy root called cassava, corn, and plantains (green cooking bananas). Farming plots are cleared from the forest and used for two or three years before being abandoned.

A Forest in Danger

Africa is losing over 9 million acres (3.5 million hectares) of tropical rain forest each year. A major cause is logging, since hardwood timbers such as iroko are valuable exports. Loggers fell other trees for making into pulp, plywood, and chipboard or for local building and fuel needs. Large areas are cleared to plant

Gentle Giants

Eastern lowland gorillas, an endangered species, are protected at the Kahuzi-Biega National Park in the Democratic Republic of the Congo. They can weigh 440 lb. (200 kg). Males may beat their chests and look fierce, but in reality they are gentle giants—and strictly vegetarian.

cash crops such as oil palm, sugarcane, or peanuts. Long years of war in central Africa have made it difficult to protect the wild animals of the forests. Hungry people often hunt this "bush meat" to stay alive, or they sell rare parrots or baby apes for money.

Check these out:

- Africa
- Ape
- Biodiversity
- Gorilla
- Human Interference
- Mbuti People
- National Park
- People of the Rain Forest

*C*onservation means "looking after" or "keeping safe" something of value. It is more than letting events take their course or leaving situations alone. It means taking positive action to protect something and safeguard its future. Conservation may aim to preserve a whole ecosystem such as a rain forest, or it may concentrate on particular elements of rain forest life, such as its bird population, its hardwood trees, or a certain animal species.

Sometimes conservation interests conflict with each other. The question may become one of conservation laws, of who owns or manages the forest.

Conservation may be a part of forest management, but the two are not necessarily the same. The aim of forest management may be to produce timber or to provide trails for hikers, to attract tourists, or to regulate farming. A management policy that allows a forest to replace its own resources as they are used is said to be sustainable.

KEY FACTS

● **About 3 percent of the world's total land area has been officially placed under protection. So far about 12 percent of these national parks and reserves include tropical rain forests.**

● **The Convention on International Trade in Endangered Species (CITES) aims to help conservation around the world by preventing the commercial exploitation of endangered plants and animals. The agreement has been signed by 148 nations.**

● **The United Nations Educational, Scientific and Cultural Organization (UNESCO) has declared more than 350 sites around the world to be biosphere reserves, large conservation areas that concentrate on scientific research, and involve local communities as much as possible.**

Finding Out the Facts

A conservation project usually starts with a scientific attempt to find out the facts and collect data about a specific area, plant, or animal. If a certain rain forest animal is endangered, then its population must be counted. The type of threat to the animal must be assessed. To find this out, it may be necessary to fit individual animals with radio collars or tags so that their movements can be tracked.

This man is not a logger but a conservationist. He is collecting seeds for reforestation in the Linhares rain forest reserve in Brazil.

Seedlings are raised to repopulate decimated forest in Brazil's Linhares reserve.

If a particular rain forest plant is under threat, the approach will be similar— scientists assess the dangers to the plant and its environment. They may need to carry out tests on the soil in order to identify a problem. Naturalists must work on the ground, often bitten by insects as they battle through dense forest. They must find out exactly how many specimens occur within a measured area, such as a large rectangle (called a quadrat). Repeating this test over and over again, naturalists can then start to estimate how many plants survive over a larger area.

If the whole rain forest is at risk, then the wider threat must be identified. Is there logging, legal or illegal? Do local farming methods destroy the forest without giving it time to recover? Is mining polluting the rivers that run through the forest? Is poverty or warfare making people move into the forest to hunt for food?

As well as working on the ground, conservationists sometimes study satellite images sent back from space. These show how people are clearing and using land and whether tropical rains are washing away soil. They may reveal highways being cut through the rain forest and telltale signs of development fringing these new roads, as well as evidence of fire. Scientists and conservationists must work out whether vegetation showing up on the pictures is original forest or just scrub that is growing back over cleared ground.

A Plan of Action
After all the scientific facts have been gathered, reported, and discussed, a conservation plan must be drawn up. It must have clear aims, a timetable of action, and sufficient funding.

IN FOCUS

The Red Lists

A World Conservation Monitoring Center based in England collects all available scientific data on plant and animal species and decides how seriously they are threatened. They publish the results in Red Lists, which register every endangered species in the world. The Center is funded by The World Conservation Union (IUCN), the United Nations Environment Programme (UNEP), and the Worldwide Fund for Nature (WWF).

Even if the plan affects just one species, conservationists must draw up a policy that takes the whole ecosystem into account, because each part of an ecosystem depends upon the others. For example, any decision to plant new trees in a forest will affect other trees and plants in the forest, the insects that pollinate them, the birds that eat those insects, and so on.

All kinds of conservation plans may be put into practice. It may be decided, for example, to plant new forest trees, to manage sections of forest in a sustainable way, or to sell plantation-grown hardwoods in order to protect wild trees. Sometimes endangered animals are captured so that they can be bred in zoos and then reintroduced into the wild. If an animal species is too numerous for a small pocket of remaining forest, it may be necessary to kill some creatures so that the rest have enough space and food to survive. This is called culling.

A naturalist studies a bird as she gathers data at the Corcovado National Park in Costa Rica. About 13 percent of Costa Rica is now protected within national parks.

Parks and Reserves

It may be decided to set part of the rain forest aside as a permanent conservation area—a reserve or a national park—to protect animals from hunters or trees from loggers. National parks all over the world carry out valuable conservation work, but such reserves are only really effective if they cover very large areas. Local people may find employment in the reserves.

However, national park authorities face many problems. People may think that conservation outside the boundaries of the reserve is no longer as important as before. They may look at the reserves as zoos, with tourists pursuing gorillas or chimpanzees almost as mercilessly as hunters did before them. Other questions arise. Should animals be allowed to pass freely over the park boundaries? Is there a need for buffer zones, a semiprotected belt of land surrounding the core reserve? There is always the danger of animal populations becoming isolated. One solution to this is to create corridors that allow animals to pass freely from one rain forest reserve to another.

Making Conservation Work

The scientific problems may be very difficult for naturalists to solve, but the political, social, and economic questions raised by conservation may be even tougher. Hunters do not poach wild animals from a reserve for fun but because they need the money. New farmers settle in the Amazon rain forest because they are already desperately poor and hope to support their families by growing crops.

Any conservation plan must take into account the needs of people living inside and outside the forest, of national governments, and of business interests. If forest dwellers can sell forest products to companies, will that help their communities survive? Like the ecosystem of a rain forest, society's needs and interests overlap and affect each other. There is no point in setting up a grand conservation plan if it will not work in practice.

IN FOCUS

Ecotourism

If you visit Central America as a tourist, you can take a tour of the rain forest canopy in Costa Rica, using ropes and platforms in the trees. In Belize you can follow a rain forest medicine trail that leads you past plant species that have medicinal value. Environment-friendly ecotourism, which has a low impact on the ecosystem, brings in money that can help fund conservation projects.

A Conservation Case Study: The Dzanga-Sangha

In 1986 the government of the Central African Republic (CAR) and the World Wildlife Fund (WWF, now the Worldwide Fund for Nature) agreed to conserve the extensive rain forests lying in the southwest of the country, the home of the Aka hunter-gatherers. Surveys revealed the region to be a haven for many endangered species, including forest elephants, lowland gorillas, and chimpanzees. Threats to the forests were identified as logging, diamond mining, hunting, road building, and clearing rain forest land for farming.

Conservation action consisted of setting up the Dzanga-Ndoki National Park and the Dzanga-Sangha Dense Forest Special Reserve. The former was an area of total protection, the latter an area where strictly limited commercial exploitation was permitted. Hunting and mining were outlawed, and park rangers were employed to patrol the conservation areas. Local people were involved in decisions and operations whenever possible. International scientists were then able to carry out more detailed surveys of the area. In 1998 alone they identified 30 new species.

Ecotourism has also been developed, bringing much-needed money into the CAR. In 1996 the American Museum of Natural History decided to re-create part of the Dzanga-Sangha in its Hall of Biodiversity, with the aim of educating and informing the public about rain forests and their conservation.

Check these out:
● Careers ● Deforestation ● Endangered Species ● Exploration and Research ● Forestry ● Human Interference ● National Park

Constrictors are the largest snakes in the world. The biggest of all is the anaconda, a boa from the tropical rivers of South America. It can grow up to 33 feet (10 m) long and can weigh over 440 pounds (200 kg).

Hunting Tactics

Many constrictors hunt by night, creeping up on their prey. By day the pupils of their eyes are like vertical slits, but at night they become wide like a cat's, letting in all possible light, which allows them to see well in the dark. The snakes also use smell and special heat sensors to find prey.

Constrictors are good swimmers. They pump air into their bodies to help them float, then let it out to sink below the surface. The anaconda lives in rivers, lying in wait for animals that come to the banks to drink. It also eats turtles and sometimes even small caimans.

Squeezed to Death

A constrictor kills its prey by coiling around it and squeezing it until it suffocates. Every time the prey exhales, the constrictor tightens its coils so that the prey cannot take as big a breath next time. In this way constrictors can kill animals larger than themselves, such as small antelope, wild pigs, and monkeys. However, constrictors prefer to eat small meals. After swallowing a large animal, they become incredibly bloated and cannot move easily.

Like all snakes, constrictors swallow their prey whole. Though they cannot chew, they have about one hundred sharply pointed teeth that curve backward for gripping. Once it has killed an animal, the snake swallows it headfirst. This prevents the prey's limbs from

KEY FACTS

● The female Indian python can warm up her eggs by as much as 13°F (7°C) when she incubates them, despite the fact that she is cold-blooded.

● A constrictor's teeth point backward into its mouth. If it bites your finger, you have to push it farther into its mouth to unhook it.

● Snakes evolved from four-footed ancestors. Pythons still have tiny hind limbs and hips under their skins.

A rainbow boa by the water's edge. Constrictors are good swimmers and can survive in flooded forests.

A young green tree python coils around a mouse to suffocate it, then pulls its mouth forward over its prey. No one knows why these pythons are red when young.

getting caught on the snake's teeth. The snake can swallow prey bigger than itself by dislocating its jaws. It moves its jaws forward over the prey, hooking its teeth in one side and then the other. Thus it pulls its mouth over its prey rather than pushing the prey down its throat. To be able to breathe with its mouth full of prey, the snake pushes its muscular windpipe forward in its mouth.

Living Incubators

Pythons lay eggs, which the female incubates for up to 60 days until they hatch. She coils herself around them, giving them the advantage of her own camouflage colors. Boas give birth to live young, and the

newborns quickly slither away out of sight. This means that the female does not have to stay and protect her offspring, so she is less at risk from other predators.

Hidden Beauty

Most constrictors rely on camouflage for defense. Many pythons have elaborate patterns of cream, black, brown, and shades of gold and orange that make them difficult to spot. The patterns break up their outlines and resemble the patterns of light and shade on the forest floor.

Some tree snakes, such as the green tree python, are bright green. Their young are bright yellow or red, not camouflaged at all. Offspring of the ringed python have bright orange and black stripes, resembling some poisonous snakes that bear these warning colors. The rainbow boa's colors change when viewed from different angles.

Their attractive skin puts many pythons and boas at risk. Large numbers are collected for the pet trade or killed for their skin. A few are eaten by local people. Others are losing their forest home to tourist resorts and deforestation.

Check these out:
● Camouflage ● Reptile ● Snake

Seeing with Heat

IN FOCUS

Constrictors that hunt mainly at night can creep up on their prey in the dark without being seen. They feed on small mammals, which are warm-blooded. Heat-sensing cells in special pits on either side of the snake's snout act like heat-seeing eyes. In pythons these pits are set in the scales, while in boas they lie between the scales.

Courtship is special behavior that helps an animal first find a partner and then persuade the new partner to mate. Animals recognize members of their own species and can also tell which sex they are by their size, color, pattern, and smell. Sight, sound, smell, and touch are all used as signals and stimulants during courtship.

KEY FACTS

● Some of the chemicals used to produce the bright colors that attract mates also protect animals from disease.

● The males and females of many species sing duets together.

● Research has shown that the frog with the loudest croak attracts the most females.

Showing Off

Birds have a poor sense of smell, but they make up for this by the splendor of their courtship displays. Male birds are often more brightly colored than females. They display their plumage to attract mates, while many females need to be well camouflaged while they sit on their eggs. The greatest showoffs of all are the birds of paradise from northern Australia and Papua New Guinea, whose courtship displays exhibit their fantastic colors and bold patterns.

Some birds, such as cocks-of-the-rock, use communal display grounds to show off their bright orange coloring and attract attention. Bowerbird males clear their own patch of ground and arrange brightly colored objects around the nest, hoping to attract a mate that way.

Females do not select mates only for their handsome appearance. Some of the chemicals used to produce bright colors in animals are also involved in resisting disease. Only healthy animals that do not need these chemicals to fight off illnesses will have enough to produce bright colors.

Not a fond embrace—these are actually two male red-eyed leaf frogs fighting for the right to court the females.

Invisible Signals

Some animals that live in dense rain forests or that are active at night use scent to attract a mate. Mammals are experts in scent and smell; most mammals have a much better sense of smell than humans do. The rain forest is full of scent trails laid down by some mammals to tell others that they are available for mating.

IN FOCUS

Flashing Flies

Fireflies are beetles that can produce light from part of their abdomen. The firefly emits flashes of light as he performs aerobatics to impress any females in the area. This is a kind of Morse code: the pattern and timing of the flashes tells the female that he is a male of the same species. She must then flash with the same timing.

Rain forest cats such as tigers and leopards produce strong-smelling chemicals in their urine. They squirt urine over bushes and tree trunks to mark their territory. Tree shrews urinate on their paws, leaving a scent trail as they scuttle along the branches.

Love Songs

Like scents, sounds are used as signals. Pigeons will fly above the forest canopy and clap their wings together to draw attention to themselves. The roars of tigers and the cries of monkeys travel a long way through the forest. Some of the noisiest animals in the rain forest are male cicadas (suh-KAE-duhs), whose metallic chirping goes on all day.

Often the male of the species makes the most noise, which not only impresses the females but also advertises his strength to rivals, helping him defend a territory to feed and breed in. This makes sure his mate and young will have enough to eat. The male curassow (KYUR-uh-soe), a turkeylike bird, makes a loud booming noise. He has a much longer windpipe than the female, who can only mumble quietly.

In forests with seasonal rains, the arrival of rain triggers a great migration of frogs to forest pools to mate and lay their eggs. As frogs converge on the pool, the chorus grows louder. Many frogs have inflatable throat sacs or cheek pouches to amplify their sound. Each species has a different kind of croak.

Too Close for Comfort

Some mates come too close for comfort. It is quite common for the female praying mantis's embrace to turn to a grip of death as, after mating, she bites off her mate's head and proceeds to eat him. The male's body will provide food for the female's developing eggs.

Check these out:
- Beetle
- Bird
- Communication
- Frog and Toad
- Insect
- Mammal

A male praying mantis (left) considers the risk of courting the egg-laden female (right). She may well take him for both mate and dinner.

Crocodylia is an order of reptiles that are superbly adapted to their amphibious way of life. This order includes crocodiles and caimans. On land crocodilians are often agile and surprisingly fast; in the water they move at great speed, using their powerful flattened tails to propel them. The bony core on the back of some species prevents most predators from sinking their teeth into the crocodilian's hide. Their scales prevent them from drying out on land and offer them a degree of protection from the sun. Since they have this watertight skin, the only way they can lose heat is to sit with their mouths agape and allow moisture to evaporate from their tongues.

Crocodilians' long jaws and sharp teeth are ideally suited to grasping prey. Crocodilians have incredibly powerful muscles to close their jaws but weak ones to open them. For that reason it is possible to tie a crocodile's mouth shut with just a piece of string.

There is little difference between crocodiles and caimans apart from the shape of their skulls and the arrangement of their teeth. In the crocodile an

KEY FACTS

● Crocodiles and caimans have been around since the time of the dinosaurs. Today's crocodiles and caimans look scarcely different from their ancestors.

● These reptiles are among the biggest predators in the rain forest. Few other animals prey upon them.

● Almost all crocodile and caiman species are considered endangered or vulnerable from hunting and habitat loss.

Hatchling caimans stay close to their mother for the first few weeks of their life. A spectacled caiman rides on its mother's back in Pantanal, Mato Grosso, Brazil.

RAIN FOREST CROCODILIANS

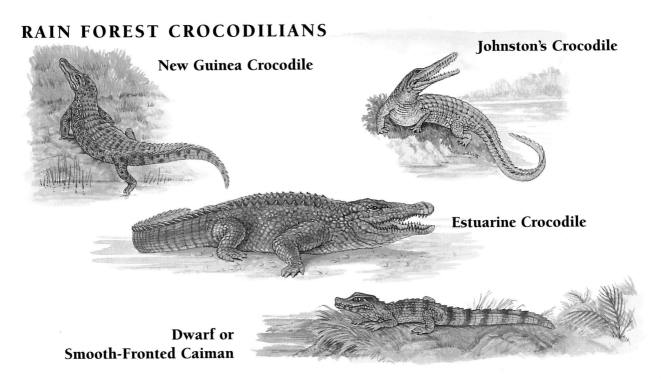

New Guinea Crocodile

Johnston's Crocodile

Estuarine Crocodile

Dwarf or Smooth-Fronted Caiman

enlarged tooth on either side of the lower jaw fits into two notches on either side of the upper jaw. In caimans all the teeth on the upper jaw overhang the lower jaw.

Crocodiles

Crocodiles are not normally associated with rain forests, but there are a few species dotted about Africa and Australasia that have become adapted to this particular environment. Equatorial western Africa is home to one of the world's smallest crocodiles, the west African dwarf crocodile. Very little is known about this species except that it is endangered. Today a determined effort to save this species involves releasing captive-bred youngsters back into the wild.

Mugger crocodiles of the Indian subcontinent are found in a variety of habitats, including rivers flowing through the dense forests. This is a large species, up to 11½ feet (3.5 m) in length with a thickset body and shortened, broad snout. They feed on both fish and animals that come down to the water to drink.

New Guinea is home to the New Guinea crocodile, which is unique to the island. This relatively small species grows to around 10 feet (3 m). Local peoples have long hunted these crocodilians for their flesh and hide. However, even the resident peoples recognize the need for caution when it comes to

IN FOCUS

People-Eating Crocodiles

The world's largest crocodile is the saltwater or estuarine crocodile. It can grow to a massive size—to nearly 23 ft. (7 m) in length and weighing 2,200 lb. (1,000 kg). Saltwater crocodiles inhabit the tropical regions of Southeast Asia and Australia. As their name suggests, as well as being found in freshwater, they often live in mangrove swamps and have even been found swimming several miles out in open seas. These are real human-eaters, as dangerous to people as great white sharks.

exploiting the crocodile population; many villages raise their own crocodiles from juveniles, feeding them on scraps of meat and leftovers. When the crocodiles grow to full size in a few years, the villagers slaughter them, reducing their need to hunt the wild population, members of which are often difficult to find.

In northern Australia the freshwater crocodile—so named to distinguish it from the only other Australian crocodile, the saltwater crocodile—is often found in rivers that flow through rain forest. Also known as Johnston's Croc, freshwater crocodiles have a slender snout and rarely exceed 6½ feet (2 m) in length. They feed mainly on fish, crustaceans, and the occasional duckling. They can often be seen sunning themselves on sandy riverbanks in forest clearings.

Caimans

Several species of caiman live in the rivers and water systems of Central and South America. The most common species is the spectacled caiman, which gets its name from the ridge of bone between its eyes. Found throughout the forested regions of Mexico and southward through Central America as far as northern Argentina, caimans inhabit lakes and ponds as well as swamps and slow-moving rivers.

Caimans are often seen basking on riverbanks or fallen logs during the day; they dive into the water at the slightest disturbance. They hunt mainly at night, when they go in search of fish, frogs, snakes, crabs, and the occasional bird or mammal. They do not take large prey because they themselves are not that large, rarely exceeding 6½ feet (2 m) long.

The caiman's breeding season normally coincides with the onset of the rains, often

Dwindling Species

Almost every one of the 22 species of crocodilians is classified as either endangered or vulnerable from hunting and habitat loss. Throughout the world crocodile farms have been set up to supply the demand for crocodile skin and meat without damaging wild, protected populations. Some of these farms also have a captive-release program to help replenish wild stocks.

between April and June. After mating in the water, the female constructs a nest not far from the water's edge. The nest is a pile of vegetable matter scraped together to a height of almost 2 feet (60 cm). She then squashes down the pile of leaves with her body as she digs a hole into the center. There she lays two or three dozen white, hard-shelled eggs, slightly longer than a chicken's egg. The caiman then covers them and leaves them to incubate, assisted by the heat generated by the rotting leaves. She remains close by to protect them until they hatch some two months later.

The hatchlings measure around 8 to 9 inches (20 to 23 cm) in length and are independent almost from birth. At first they feed on aquatic insects, snails, and small fish, progressing to larger prey as they grow. It takes them seven or eight years to reach a size when they can start to breed. Unfortunately huge numbers of baby caimans are caught, killed, and stuffed for sale to tourists.

Large numbers of baby caimans also make their way into the pet trade, especially in North America. There, they quickly outgrow their accommodation and pose real problems for their owners. Zoos may take some, but many have been released into the swamps and rivers of Florida, where they have become well established and may pose a threat to the local wildlife.

The largest caiman in South America is the black caiman. It is the only species that could be considered really dangerous to people. It can reach almost 16 feet (5 m) in length, but a more usual size is 11½ to 13 feet (3.5 to 4 m). It inhabits the rivers of Brazil and Peru, where it lies in wait for mammals such as the capybara to come into range. Black caimans also eat fish, terrapins, and snakes and are responsible for several human deaths a year. Although they spend most of their time in rivers, they often migrate overland to lakes where they nest and where their young will get a good head start in life before moving into the rivers themselves. These youngsters have to be very wary, though, as black caimans are often cannibalistic, eating members of their own species.

One of the smallest species of caiman is the smooth-fronted caiman of Brazil that reaches a maximum length of nearly 5 feet (1.5 m), although it is usually much smaller. These caimans inhabit the smaller rivers of the Amazon but are unusual in that they often spend long periods on land in the rain forest, well away from water. They lay only a small number of eggs in nests hidden in the forest.

A mugger, or marsh, crocodile sits in shallow water. Marsh crocodiles inhabit the rivers of India and neighboring countries.

Check these out:
- Carnivore - Reptile

Crustaceans are small animals whose body parts are covered in a shell made of a chalky substance called chitin (KIE-tehn). They include crabs, lobsters, crayfish, shrimps, wood lice (sow bugs or pill bugs), copepods (KOE-puh-pahds), and water fleas. Crustaceans have two pairs of feelers, at least five pairs of jointed legs, and a pair of jawlike mandibles. Tiny mouthparts that look like pairs of little legs put food into their mouths.

Crustacean bodies are made up of many small sections, called segments, each with a separate shell on the outside, seen clearly in wood lice. There is no shell between the segments, so they can bend their bodies easily. However, in crabs, crayfish, and shrimps, several segments join together to form a rigid shield structure covering the head and chest. A crab's abdomen is curled right under its body and ends just below its mouth.

Crustaceans breathe through delicate structures called gills, which must be kept moist. Some wood lice have tubes in their legs for breathing air as well.

Water Creatures

Rain forest pools and streams are full of tiny swimming crustaceans, such as water fleas and copepods, many less than one eighth of an inch (2 mm) long. These tiny creatures beat their feelers to swim. Freshwater shrimp scavenge in

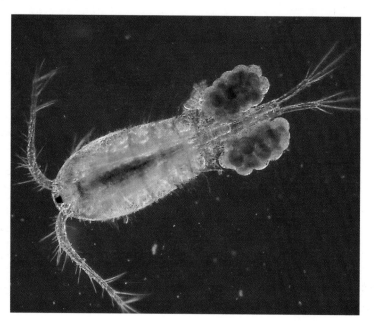

the mud and under rocks for the remains of dead plants and animals. Shrimp have little paddles called swimmerets on their rear segment for swimming. All these animals use rows of bristles on their legs or mouthparts to filter tiny pieces of food from the water.

A copepod as viewed under a microscope. Copepods filter even tinier plants and animals from the water.

KEY FACTS

● **The huge coconut crab can scale coconut palms 60 ft. (18 m) tall, using the sharp tips of its legs like spikes for climbing. Its powerful pincers cut coconuts from the trees.**

● **Hermit crabs save themselves the effort of producing a thick shell by tucking their bodies into the abandoned shells of snails.**

● **When in danger, pill bugs roll up into a ball. The chalky plates on their back protect their softer underparts from attack.**

A red land crab has large pincers for display, defense, and feeding. Its little black eyes are on short stalks.

A couple of weeks after fertilization, the eggs are ready to hatch, and the females wade into the sea to release the larvae.

Garbage Collectors

Surprisingly, many rain forests have large populations of crabs. Important scavengers, they clear rotting debris on the forest floor and help tear up the bodies of dead plants and animals so that fungi and bacteria can move in and break them down. Land crabs live in deep burrows in the forest floor, where the air stays moist.

Some of these crabs are very large. The Caribbean land crab grows up to 6 inches (15 cm) across its shell. It uses its large pincers to defend itself.

Water Babies

Crustaceans lay eggs that hatch into tiny, swimming larvae, which look quite unlike their parents. As they grow, the larvae shed their shell from time to time, each time becoming more like an adult crustacean.

Land crabs have one big problem—they have to go back to the sea to release their eggs so that the newborn larvae have salt water to live in. At certain times of the year, land crabs migrate in great swarms to the coast, often traveling many miles to find mates on the beach. They may even go through people's homes if they happen to be in the way. The female crabs may be carrying 20,000 to 100,000 eggs each.

Litter Bugs

Wood lice are familiar creatures from many people's homes and yards, but they are also common on the forest floor, where they feed on mosses, fungi, bark, and dead and decaying plant material. Some have spikes on their back that protect them, especially when they are rolled up. The spikes also help them dig into the soil.

Wood lice dry out easily; they tend to be active at night, when the air is cooler and moister. By day they hide under leaves or stones or in crevices in tree bark. They cannot see well and tend to avoid the light.

Check these out:
● Bromeliad ● Decomposer
● Fish ● Flooding

Treetop Crabs

IN FOCUS

Some tiny crabs live in the little pools that collect among the leaves of bromeliads (broe-MEE-lee-ads) high among the treetops. The female crab first removes rotting leaves and other debris in the pool and then lays her eggs. Once the eggs hatch, the larvae look like miniature adult crabs. Their mother stays for two months to defend them against enemies such as dragonfly larvae. She catches even tinier animals among the bromeliad leaves to feed her young.

Decomposition is an important part of every life cycle. It is nature's way of recycling nutrients from dead organisms to make them available for living organisms. Some decomposition takes place very quickly, while some can take months, even years, to occur, especially in the case of hard, dense substances such as bone.

Dead plants and dead animals usually have separate sets of decomposers; only bacteria and fungi (FUN-jie) are not choosy about the material they consume.

KEY FACTS

● **Decomposers play a vital role in every food chain. Without them we would be knee-deep in dead plants and animals.**

● **Some earthworms that feed on dead leaves can grow to 6½ ft. (2 m) long.**

Plant Decomposers

Rain forest plants are evergreen in that they do not have periods where the plants are completely leafless. They constantly produce new leaves and shed old ones throughout the year. Plant material—seeds, seed pods, fruits, and leaves—constantly falls to the forest floor. Many animals feed on the dead leaves.

Millipedes consume large amounts of leaf litter and in doing so produce large volumes of rich droppings which fertilize the forest plants. Most millipedes are nocturnal, but some species are active during the day. They rarely feed on living plant material, as their jaws are simply not strong enough.

Earthworms emerge from their burrows in the forest soil at night or after heavy rains. They too feed on dead leaves and produce copious amounts of waste, called worm casts, that fertilize the soil. Some of these earthworms can grow as large as 6½ feet (2 m) long and as thick as a person's thumb.

It's not just leaves that need decomposing. Twigs, branches, and eventually whole trees hit the forest floor. These are jobs for termites, which munch their way through wood at incredible speed. Woody material is very difficult to digest because it is composed mainly of cellulose. The termites have overcome this: bacteria living in their gut break down the cellulose into a more digestible form.

The giant pill millipede can stretch to 3 in. (8 cm) and feeds on dead plant material.

Some fungi attack insects before they are dead. This parasitic fungus from Peru kills its host slowly, then produces spore-laden fruiting bodies.

Bacteria and Fungi

Bacteria feed on dead organic matter by extracellular digestion. They secrete enzymes onto the food that dissolve it into nutrients. The bacteria then absorb these through their cell walls.

The main part of a fungus consists of numerous branching threads, called hyphae, that spread throughout soil and leaf litter. They too feed on dead matter by extracellular digestion, secreting enzymes and then absorbing digested food.

Animal Decomposers

When an animal dies, it usually drops to the forest floor. Scavengers are attracted to the body to feed on the flesh and bones.

Carrion beetles are attracted to the corpse, and both they and their larvae eat the flesh. So too do fly larvae, maggots that appear within days of the death. Large corpses may attract scavengers such as vultures that can detect the scent of an animal's corpse through the canopy as they fly over the forest. Forest tortoises often pick over animal remains, as do freshwater crabs and some lizards. Often all that is left are some of the larger bones. Any remnants of flesh that remain are usually disposed of by microscopic bacteria and fungi.

Animal droppings are also decomposed. The male dung beetle collects the dung and rolls it into a ball. The female lays her eggs in the ball of dung then buries it in the soil, thus protecting the offspring and providing them with a plentiful food supply.

Check these out:
- Bacteria ● Beetle ● Ecology ● Ecosystem
- Food Web ● Forest Floor ● Fungus
- Millipede ● Termite ● Worm

IN FOCUS

Decomposers in Conservation

In eastern Africa stands an old quarry that the owners were determined to return to a more pleasant natural state. They managed to establish some trees and then introduced a large number of giant millipedes. The millipedes eagerly devoured the fallen leaves and produced rich droppings, perfect for the cultivation of more plants. Now, only twenty years later, the quarry provides a lush, fertile wildlife habitat.

Deer belong to a group of animals called true ruminants. They have complex stomachs where plant material ferments. Like cows, deer chew their food only a few times before swallowing it. The vegetable matter is then partially digested before the animal brings it back up from its stomach and chews it some more. Then it swallows it again, so aiding digestion. This is known as chewing the cud and explains why deer are often seen chewing when they have not bent down and eaten anything. It is an important survival strategy because it means that the deer need spend only a small amount of time feeding and exposed to predators. It can then chew its food in the hidden depths of the forest.

The antlers of adult male deer set them apart from other members of the group. Unlike horns, antlers are shed and regrown every year. Depending on the species, antlers range in size from simple spikes to enormous coatrack-type structures like those on the red deer. Male deer use these antlers in combat

KEY FACTS

● **There are about 36 species of deer worldwide. At least 5 species live in rain forest regions. Several other species occupy other habitats around the fringes of the rain forest.**

● **Muntjacs weigh no more than 38 lb. (17 kg) and are not much larger than a medium-sized dog.**

The antlers of this male sambar are just starting to grow. Sambars inhabit the rain forests of India.

A Special Partnership

Axis deer are often found feeding alongside groups of langur monkeys. The deer graze underneath trees where the monkeys are feeding. Not only do deer eat large numbers of leaves dropped by monkeys (which are very messy eaters), but they also warn each other of approaching predators. Deer have an excellent sense of smell, while the monkeys benefit from a high vantage point. Should a leopard or tiger approach, either the deer or monkeys can sense the predator and all can escape.

inhabitant, the axis deer is usually seen only when it ventures out into the forest clearings or onto riverbanks.

The male carries a fine set of antlers, each with three points, or tines. He may reach a height of nearly 3 feet (1 m) at the shoulder and weigh 165 pounds (75 kg). The female is much smaller and has no antlers.

Axis deer feed mainly in the cooler parts of the day, in early morning and late afternoon. Browsers and grazers, they feed on the fresh grass with other males, and they often get damaged. Renewing them means they can start off every rutting season in perfect fighting condition.

Deer are normally animals of open plains, grass, and woodlands, where they can watch out for danger or rivals. However, a few species graze in some of the world's tropical rain forests.

Axis Deer

The lush tropical rain forests of India and Sri Lanka are the habitat of the axis deer, or chital. This medium-sized species of deer wears a rich brown coat covered in white spots; in fact it is sometimes known as the spotted deer. A shy forest that grows in the open areas of the forest and browse on a whole range of shrubs and trees, taking only the youngest, most tender shoots.

The axis deer is a social animal, living in herds that may reach over one hundred members. The majority of these groups are composed of female deer and their young and just a handful of large, mature males. The immature males form bachelor groups on their own until they are big enough to fight for a place in a mixed herd. The favorite prey of tigers and leopards, axis deer are shy, wary animals, ready to bolt at the slightest hint of danger. They swim well and often take to the water to make their escape.

remain still and hidden in dense vegetation, where they are well camouflaged. The female will visit to feed her offspring and remain close by. After a week or two, the fawns are strong and confident enough to follow their mothers and join the herd. They will be suckled for nearly two months.

Brockets

Brockets inhabit the rain forests of Central and South America from sea level up to over 13,000 feet (4,000 m). One species, the red brocket, is found in the lush rain forests of southern Mexico to northern Argentina. In size it is very similar to the axis deer, standing about 30 inches (76 cm) at the shoulder, but it is a little lighter, at around 100 to 110 pounds (45 to 50 kg).

The brocket is a uniform reddish brown and is difficult to spot when it stands motionless in the gloom of the forest. The underside of the tail is white and is used to signal danger to the other deer. The males do not possess the large, impressive antlers sported by other deer but instead have small, simple spikes.

Brocket live solitary lives and only occasionally form small family groups of a male, a female, and her young of the previous year. Known to be active at all times of night and day, they are constantly

However, this is not always a good idea, as the rivers where they live are inhabited by large mugger crocodiles, which are partial to axis deer.

Axis deer breed year-round. The males fight each other during the rut, fierce contests of strength during which the stags use their antlers to full effect. The fawns are born about seven months after mating and resemble their parents in color. They can walk from their first day of life, but as is common with other deer, they on the alert for danger and either freeze or bolt when threatened. Brockets and their young may plunge into lakes and streams to escape from jaguars, one of their main predators. Although jaguars swim well, they find it difficult to track the deer once they have entered the water.

Brockets feed on a wide range of vegetable matter, such as grasses and the leaves, fruits, and seeds of shrubs and vines: hard, dry fruits during the dry season, and rich, fleshy fruits during the rains. They will also eat mushrooms and toadstools.

Like the axis deer, the flesh of the brocket is highly prized by humans throughout its range. However, tracking a brocket down and killing it is not an easy task.

Sambars

The sambar (SAHM-buhr) is found in the forests of the Philippines, Indonesia, India, and Burma. It is not a creature of the densest rain forest but prefers areas with spaces in the undergrowth between the trees. Its large, branched antlers would catch on tree limbs in the densest part of the forest. It is quite a large deer: an adult can weigh over 440 pounds (200 kg). The sambar is normally darkish brown with a lighter brown underside.

An Endangered Deer

A native of the forests of the Philippines, the Visayan spotted deer is one of the rarest and least known species of rain forest deer in the world. A dark brown deer, with light brown spots and a pale underside and tail, it is similar to the sambar, to which it is closely related.

The Visayan spotted deer is highly secretive and its numbers have been much reduced by hunting and logging. It is classified as an endangered species and could become extinct in the next few years unless drastic measures are taken in order to save it.

Check these out:
- Africa
- Camouflage
- Herbivore
- Indonesia
- Mammal

IN FOCUS

A Dog-Sized Deer

The muntjac is a very small species of rain forest deer. Reaching a shoulder height of scarcely 23 in. (60 cm) and a weight of 38 lb. (17 kg), it is not much bigger than a medium-sized dog. It lives in forests with plenty of undergrowth, where it can disappear from view in the blink of an eye. Muntjacs have tiny spiked antlers, but the male's canine teeth are large and form tusks. They feed mainly on herbs, leaves, fungi, fruit, and even tree bark.

Deforestation is the disappearance of natural forest cover from the land. This is sometimes a natural process, perhaps the result of the climate becoming drier. However, deforestation is more often the result of human activities, such as felling trees for timber or burning them to clear land for agriculture; allowing herds of goats or cattle to eat saplings; or polluting land, air, or water supplies.

Disappearing Forests

Nowhere has the destruction of forests been more pronounced than in tropical rain forests. In Southeast Asia, Thailand is losing 8 percent of its rain forest each year; the Philippines, 5 percent. In Africa, Nigeria is losing 14 percent each year; Ivory Coast 16 percent; Madagascar, 8 percent. In the Americas, Ecuador and Mexico are losing 4 percent of their rain forest annually, while Brazil, Bolivia, and Colombia are losing over 2 percent.

Tropical rain forests are mostly located in poor and developing countries where there is great pressure on governments to repay international debts and improve their economies. Developed countries offer a rich market for precious tropical hardwoods and native plants that can be used for medicines. In the short term, clearing the rain forest seems to offer all kinds of local benefits. However, the long-term problems are serious, and they affect not just local people but the planet as a whole.

Short-Term Gains

The most obvious reason for the destruction of the forests is the felling of trees for timber. Tropical forests produce valuable hardwoods such as teak, iroko,

KEY FACTS

● **The world's rain forests are reduced by an area the size of Wyoming every year.**

● **At the present rate of deforestation, between 5 and 10 percent of all rain forest animal and plant species will become extinct every 10 years.**

● **Unless the destruction of the forests is brought under control, within 20 years the only large surviving rain forests will be in the Amazon and Congo Basins.**

● **Within the next one hundred years, there may be no tropical forest at all left in the world.**

A satellite image of the Rondonia region of Amazonia. The light brown areas are evidence of deforestation.

mahogany, and ebony, used for furniture or ornaments. Softwoods too may be used to make furniture or fittings (small wooden parts), provide plywood and chipboard, or to make into pulp for paper mills.

Mud and broken branches are all that remain after the clearance of forest in Johor State, Malaysia.

IN FOCUS

Home of the Indri

The African island of Madagascar has lost 93 percent of its original rain forest. Soil has been washed away, leaving only barren rock. The survival of no fewer than 127 animal species is threatened. These species include the indri, a type of lemur. The indri once lived over a much wider area, but even its current range is shrinking year by year as a result of slash-and-burn farming, clearing local trees for fuel, and illegal logging. Scientists are using satellites in space to survey the forest, hoping to save the indri from extinction.

Another way the forests are stripped is through general clearance by saw and machete or by deliberate or accidental fires. Forest peoples may use the slash-and-burn method of cultivation: clearing a plot of land for growing crops, then letting it grow again when the soil is exhausted. However, forest is often cleared on a larger scale to make way for plantations of teak or rubber trees, for fields of cash crops such as bananas or sugarcane, or for large cattle ranches with an average of over 59,000 acres (24,000 ha) each. Some ranches in Brazil, for example, are as large as 1,400,000 acres (560,000 ha).

As the human population rises, cities, towns, and villages all grow bigger and spread across the countryside. Rain forest springs and streams are diverted to supply people with water. Dams are built across rivers to provide the cities with hydroelectric power. Insect-infested wetlands are drained. Airstrips are cut from the forest. Soon prospectors arrive, looking for gold, copper, iron ore, or oil, and rivers through the forest become polluted with chemicals released in mining.

Long-Term Losses

Rain forests are complex and complicated ecosystems. Every part of them, whether animal, vegetable, or mineral, depends on the other. Tall hardwood trees do not grow back quickly, and once a few links in this fragile network are broken, the whole system collapses. The loss of a particular tract of rain forest may result in the elimination of countless species.

When trees and undergrowth are burned down, the air is filled with smoke, adding a dense layer of nitrous oxide, carbon dioxide, and other gases to the earth's atmosphere. These gases reflect warmth back to the earth's surface, making it overheat. The result of such global warming could be a worldwide rise in sea levels, violent storms, flooding, land turning to desert, and further deforestation. Already blankets of smog, created by burning fires in the rain forests, have darkened skies over vast areas of Southeast Asia.

Once a section of rain forest has been cleared, the soil quickly becomes thin and poor. Without its covering of dead leaves, it loses its natural compost. Without roots to trap moisture, the soil may dry, crack, and crumble. The soil may be washed away by heavy rains or blown by the wind. New farms often turn to dust and have to be abandoned. New dams, often built at great public expense, may simply be blocked by river mud. The rain forest may vanish forever, and nothing permanent will have been gained.

IN FOCUS

Roads to Ruin

Thousands of miles of roads have been cut through the South and Central American forests. Roads are often seen as symbols of the modern world, of economic progress. However, they bring ruin to rain forests. They bring in settlers, loggers, farmers, hunters, and miners. Their construction destroys valuable plants and prevents the free movement of animals. The roads often collapse in the heavy rains, causing landslides and flooding.

In fact much has been lost already. Rain forests are rich environments, and scientists believe that they could be home to over half of all the world's plant and animal species. Most of these living things cannot survive outside a rain forest environment and will become extinct if it is destroyed. Their loss might well be regretted by humans, for many tropical plants already provide us with useful medicines and valuable foods. New or previously unknown plant and animal species are being discovered all the time in the threatened forests.

Impact on Humans

The peoples who have always lived in the rain forests, such as the Yanomami of South America or the Mbuti of central Africa, pose little threat to the future of the forests. They hunt and fish but do not threaten the ecosystem as a whole. Rather, they form part of it. Their farming is on a small scale, producing just enough for their own needs or for the local market.

However, deforestation often devastates the lives of indigenous people. The people are no longer able to hunt, their rivers and water supplies are poisoned, their lands are seized. Ranchers, miners, and other settlers may murder them or pass on diseases to which they have no resistance. To the outside world the forest dwellers become little more than a "primitive" curiosity, to be gazed at by passing tourists. Yet these peoples are really experts who understand the richness of the rain forests.

Stop the Logging?

In 1992 the United Nations Conference on Environment and Development called an Earth Summit in Rio de Janeiro, Brazil. Deforestation was high on the agenda.

Some of the poorer countries believed they should be allowed to use their own forest resources as they felt best. The world's richer nations proposed an agreement that would eventually lead to a worldwide treaty on deforestation. However, they were not prepared to offer compensation to the poorer countries for their loss of income or to cancel international debts. In the years since 1992, the nations have met again and again, but no agreement has yet been reached.

Many countries do have restrictions on logging and the import and export of hardwoods. There are many excellent conservation, forest management, and replanting projects. Even some poorer nations, such as Uganda, have made deforestation a key issue. Often, however, rain forest regions are remote and hard to police, so illegal logging is difficult to prevent. In the developed countries, timber suppliers have agreed to label the source of hardwoods. Consumers have boycotted many items that are linked with rain forest destruction. However, the forests are still disappearing at an alarming rate.

Signs of "progress." Grids of roads and housing spill across rain forest land near Manaus, capital of Amazonas state in Brazil.

Check these out:

- Carbon Cycle
- Cattle Ranching
- Clear-Cutting
- Erosion
- lobal Warming
- Human Interference
- Logging
- Madagascar
- Reforestation

Adisease is a condition that affects living organisms in a negative way. Different diseases can be identified by the symptoms they cause. Some diseases, such as the common cold, are infectious, which means they can be passed from one organism to another. Infectious diseases are caused by parasites, such as bacteria, viruses, and worms, that enter the affected organism through air passages, skin cuts, and so on. Other diseases are noninfectious. Diseases have many causes, including inheritance (for example, arthritis) and poisoning.

Many diseases are common only in certain areas of the world because of the climate, the geography, and the animals and plants that live there. These are called endemic diseases. The major diseases that occur in the rain forest are typical tropical diseases, such as malaria, schistosomiasis, and yellow fever.

KEY FACTS

● **Malaria is often fatal, killing about 2 million people every year.**

● **Since the 1980s, about one in five Yanomami people have died from introduced diseases.**

● **The antimalarial drug quinine comes from the bark of the cinchona tree.**

Malaria

Malaria is caused by a parasitic, single-celled organism called plasmodium. It affects humans, apes, and monkeys. The organism is spread by mosquitoes that suck in the infected blood from one person and then bite another healthy person, passing the disease on. Key symptoms include fever and chills, shaking, and anemia. Malaria is often fatal, killing about 2 million people every year.

Schistosomiasis and Onchocerciasis

Schistosomiasis, or bilharziasis, is caused by parasitic worms called blood flukes that live in the victim's blood vessels. Its symptoms are coughing, fever, skin rashes, and liver damage. The female worm can lay thousands of eggs every day; these are passed out of the victim's body. If they reach fresh water, they hatch, and the worm larvae swim until they find a snail. They grow inside the snail, then swim until they find a mammal and enter the body.

Another tropical disease caused by parasitic worms is onchocerciasis, or river blindness, which is spread by blackflies that breed in rivers.

An anopheline mosquito feeding on a human. This species is known to carry malaria. It has sunk its long, sharp mouthparts into the skin.

People of the rain forest occasionally receive treatment from doctors who administer Western-style medicine.

Yellow Fever

A virus spread by mosquitoes causes yellow fever, a disease that affects humans, monkeys, and some small mammals. Yellow fever causes aches, fever, and vomiting. Often fatal, it is endemic in the Amazon Basin and central Africa.

Treatment and Prevention

Most tropical diseases can be treated with modern drugs that kill the parasites and relieve the symptoms. However, in poorer nations these drugs are expensive and not readily available to millions of people. Indigenous rain forest people use hundreds of different natural drugs produced from plants for treating disease. Most famous of these is the antimalarial drug quinine, which comes from the bark of the cinchona tree.

Preventing a disease is far better than curing it. People have an immune system that fights disease. They gain natural immunity to many diseases after catching them for the first time but can also be immunized artificially by vaccination.

The spread of parasitic diseases such as malaria and schistosomiasis can be prevented by removing the source of the disease—for example, by filling in the stagnant pools where mosquitoes breed. However, human activities in the rain forest often make the situation worse. Stagnant water is created by mining and dam building and in new settlements built for mine workers.

Check these out:

- Bacteria
- Bug
- Hydroelectricity
- Kaluli People
- Kayapo People
- Kuna People
- Medicinal Plant
- Mining
- Mosquito
- Parasite
- People of the Rain Forest
- Resettlement
- Yanomami People

IN FOCUS

Death by European Disease

Since their first contacts with Europeans in the 16th century, indigenous rain forest peoples have been affected by diseases brought by Westerners. Thousands have died from diseases to which they have no natural immunity, such as measles, influenza, smallpox, and even the common cold. For example, since gold miners moved onto the land occupied by the Yanomami people in Brazil in the late 1980s, about one in five Yanomamis have died from introduced diseases.

Dolphins are mammals with large brains and streamlined, fishlike bodies. Despite being warm-blooded, they spend their lives under water and must surface to breathe. Dolphins are fast and agile predators, often hunting in groups. Most dolphins live in the sea, but some tropical rivers have their own freshwater dolphins. The boto, or pink river dolphin, lives in the rivers of South America, while susus (SOO-soos) swim in the Indus and Ganges Rivers of India, Bangladesh, and Pakistan.

Shy creatures, river dolphins live in muddy water. The largest species is the boto, which grows up to 8 feet 4 inches (2.6 m) long. With their long, narrow snouts, river dolphins probe in the mud in search of small fish and crustaceans. Large numbers of pointed teeth help them grip slippery fish.

All river dolphins, except the boto, are nearly blind. Their tiny eyes can detect only the direction and brightness of light. Instead the dolphins send out a series of clicking sounds that bounce off objects in the water, a process known as echolocation. The echos tell the dolphin the location of these objects.

River dolphins are rarely killed by local people. However, all over the Tropics, rivers are being dammed to produce hydroelectric power. This prevents fish from reaching their breeding grounds, so there are fewer fish for dolphins to catch. It also prevents the dolphins from traveling far in search of food.

Threats to River Dolphins

Waste from factories, sewage from towns, and pesticides from farmland are polluting many rivers. For example, over 2,200 tons (2,000 metric tons) of mercury enter the Amazon from gold mines each year. Along the banks of the Ganges River, 2,750 tons (2,500 metric tons) of pesticides and over 1,300,000 tons (1,200,000 metric tons) of fertilizers are used. This makes both fish and dolphins sick and hampers their ability to reproduce.

Increased river traffic is also a threat. Fishing nets and lines trap river dolphins. Boats cause injury and death as propellers hit dolphins. The noise of boats may also upset their echolocation system.

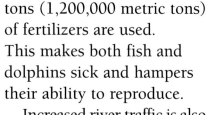

The Amazon river dolphin, or boto, has small eyes and poor eyesight. It uses its long snout to feel for food in the mud.

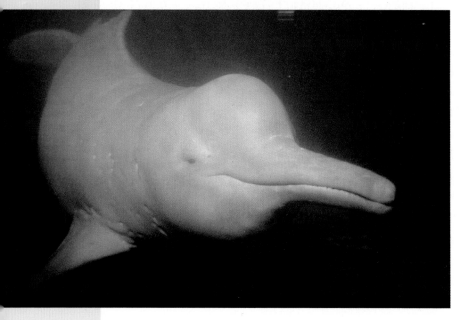

Check these out:
- Endangered Species
- Fish ● Hydroelectricity
- Mammal ● River

Dormancy is the ability of a plant to wait until conditions are right for it to grow. It is most common in seeds or spores, which wait for warmth or moisture to trigger their germination, but in the rain forest young trees can also be dormant, waiting for a light gap to appear.

Surrounded by ferns, Sitka spruce saplings, specialists at growing in dim light, put down their roots in the mosses covering a nurse log in the Hoh Valley temperate rain forest, Washington.

The floor of the rain forest is dark, shaded by the closed canopy as much as 130 feet (40 m) above. Only one percent of the light that falls on the canopy reaches the ground. Not many plants can grow in such dim conditions; a few mosses and ferns are usually the only plants at ground level. However, under them lie the seeds of the forest plants, waiting for their chance to germinate.

Reaching the Light

Tropical plant seeds germinate when the temperature is right and when there's enough moisture, provided their seed coats are not too tough. Some must wait until their outer coats have rotted slightly so that the shoot can escape. When these seeds germinate on the dark forest floor, though, they still have a struggle ahead of them. They must wait for a light gap to appear, usually when an ancient tree dies or when a wind storm throws some of the tallest trees to the ground. The sunlight falling through the gap triggers some seeds to germinate by warming the soil.

Some seedlings have an advantage over their neighbors because they germinate and put down their first small roots on a nurse log. This is the long-dead trunk of a fallen tree, covered in mosses and other small plants that hold enough moisture for seedlings to grow. Raised above the forest floor, these seedlings have a head start in the race toward the light. When they finally reach full size, their roots betray their early days, typically growing in a hoop shape, looking bowlegged from straddling the nurse log in their infancy. This generation of dormant plants, waiting on the forest floor for their elders to fall, is vital for the regeneration of the forest when wind or fire creates gaps in the canopy.

Check these out:
● Forest Floor ● Leaf ● Light Gap ● Plant ● Seed ● Shade Toleration

Dragonfly

Among the fastest and most agile of all insects, dragonflies are efficient hunters, with slender bodies and enormous eyes that cover most of their head and enable them to spot mosquitoes and other small insects in flight. Big, shiny wings allow these insects to change direction instantly and give chase.

There are two main groups of dragonflies: the true dragonflies and the damselflies. True dragonflies have stouter bodies than the damselflies, and they always rest with their wings outstretched; they cannot bring them together over their body. Dragonflies catch most of their food in midair, scooping it up in a sort of basket formed by their spiky front legs. They also snatch resting insects. Damselflies are altogether more delicate insects, with slender bodies, and they often rest with their wings together. Damselflies fly more slowly than the true dragonflies and get most of their food by plucking insects from leaves.

Both groups normally grow up in water, where the young stages, called nymphs, are fiercely carnivorous. The lower jaw, called the mask, carries strong spines; it shoots out at high speed to impale worms and other small creatures.

Breeding Sites

Many different kinds of dragonflies, including some of the world's largest species, live in the rain forests, where there are plenty of mosquitoes and other insects for them to catch throughout the year. However, breeding can be a problem in the forests because there are not many ponds. Some species breed in the rivers, but others have to

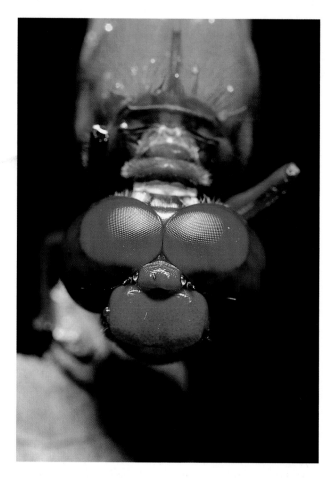

Some of the thousands of tiny lenses that make up the eyes can be seen in this photograph of an aeshnid dragonfly from the rain forests of Costa Rica.

154

use smaller bodies of water, including the pools that form in the forks of trees and in the bark crevices of fallen trees.

The water that collects in the leaf bases of bromeliads (broe-MEE-lee-ads) and other plants provides crucial breeding sites for rain forest dragonflies and especially for damselflies. The insects most commonly use those niches on or near the ground. The damselflies that breed in these small pools have longer and more slender bodies than their relatives, so they can lay their eggs in narrower crevices.

Dragonflies living in rain forests with only seasonal rains manage to survive because they pass the drier months in the adult state. While they lay their eggs on damp ground, the eggs do not hatch until the rains return and flood the ground. Most unusual of all, however, are the dragonflies whose nymphs have given up living in the water altogether. They survive perfectly well among the damp, decaying leaves on the forest floor. These nonaquatic species live mainly in the forests of Hawaii and a few other tropical islands.

IN FOCUS

The Giant Damselfly

The world's largest damselfly lives in Central American rain forests. With a wingspan of about 7 in. (18 cm) and a body of about 5 in. (13 cm) long, it is bigger than most true dragonflies, although its body is still very slender. The giant damselfly breeds in the small pools of water that collect in the bases of bromeliad plants. Its nymphs feed on the tadpoles and mosquito larvae that live in these pools.

Hovering on its big wings, the damselfly plucks spiders from their webs and eats them. Its wings are thin and transparent, with just a patch of color near the tip, and the insect is almost invisible in flight. All that can be seen are little flashes of color from the wing tips as the insect drifts through the forest at dusk. The native forest people once believed that these ghostlike insects were the spirits of their dead relatives.

Check these out:

- Bromeliad
- Insect
- Insectivore

Dyak (DIE-ak) is the collective name given to the aboriginal inhabitants of the island of Borneo—those who lived there before people from Malaysia and China, and later from Java, moved in. The Dyaks live mainly in the south and west, in the Indonesian area of Kalimantan. Some other Dyak groups live in Sabah and Sarawak, which are part of Malaysia. The Dyak population today is about 2 million people, out of a total population of 35 million on the island of Borneo. They live mainly in the forests along the banks of large rivers.

KEY FACTS

● **Dyak people were the first to live on the island of Borneo.**

● **Dyaks hunt birds and monkeys using long blowguns.**

● **Once feared as headhunters, the Dyaks are now admired for their deep understanding of the forests.**

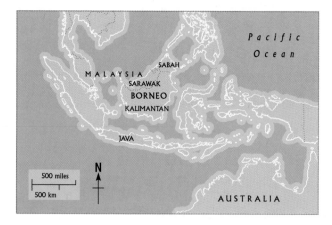

Dyak Tribes

The Dyak peoples are usually divided into six groups: the Penan, Klemantan, and Kenyah, which are said to be the oldest on the island, and the Kayan, Murut, and Iban, who arrived later, at least five hundred years ago, though exactly when and from where is unknown. The Dyaks do not pay much attention to group divisions. The only really distinct group is the Iban (EE-bahn), sometimes called the Sea Dyaks, who live around the coast and were once feared as pirates and headhunters.

The rest of the Dyaks live inland, fishing and hunting in the forest and growing rice in small clearings on the hillsides. They fish like people elsewhere—with spears,

A Dyak hunter from the Penan group sharpens his spear beside one of the forest streams that supply much of their food.

Roofed with a mixture of thatch and wooden shingles, the longhouse is the center of a Dyak community.

Dyak Homes

A typical Dyak community consists of about two hundred people living together in a single longhouse. Children stay with their parents until they are married; boys go with their new wife to live in her village. They do not think of themselves as members of any particular group but more as part of their local community.

nets, and traps—but they have a unique hunting weapon, the blowgun, which they still use to hunt monkeys and birds. More than 3 feet (1 m) long, in skilled hands a blowpipe can fire a poisoned dart 33 feet (10 m) up into the trees. While the men go hunting or fishing, the women gather food in the forest and collect berries and herbs for use in medicine. Ethnobotanists today are learning about new medicines from the Dyaks. Skilled artisans, the Dyaks weave fine cloth from plant fibers and forge iron tools and weapons.

The headhunting that so horrified the first Dutch explorers in the 17th century was part of the territorial battles between neighboring communities trying to keep control of a large enough area of forest to feed their people. The practice faded out under the Dutch colonial administration (which came to an end in 1949). However, the village dances and feasts that were once associated with it still go on, more for recreation—and to thrill tourists—than to terrify neighbors. The first group to give up headhunting was the much-feared Iban, probably because, living by the sea, they had the most contact with people from outside.

As logging companies try to take over their forest home, the Dyak peoples are under pressure to give up their old ways. In spite of attempts by the government to resettle them in "modern" communities, most Dyaks would prefer to continue living as their ancestors did.

IN FOCUS

Bridges from Bark

Living among dense hillside forests that are divided by swift rivers in deep gorges, the Dyak peoples are good at making suspension bridges. They use bamboo tied together with fibers made from tree bark. The bridges look flimsy, swaying high above the water, but people use them every day.

Check these out:
- Homes in the Rain Forest
- Hunter-Gatherer • People of the Rain Forest • Resettlement

Eagles are the largest birds of prey. Their broad wings enable them to soar for hours without flapping as they search for their prey below with unrivaled eyesight. Their powerful talons and sharp, hooked beaks are perfect for killing and tearing their prey.

Eagles are usually pictured soaring over mountainsides or plains, hunting their prey under the wide open sky, not as forest birds. However, there are three great forest eagles: the crowned eagle, sometimes called "the king of African birds;" the harpy eagle of Central and South America, which is the largest eagle in the world; and the monkey-eating eagle of the Philippines, which is only slightly smaller, with a wingspan of nearly 6½ feet (2 m). The crowned eagle is the best-known of the three, but the lives of all three forest eagles are similar. These eagles hunt just under the forest canopy, where there is plenty of space between the trees for them to maneuver.

KEY FACTS

● **Of the three rain forest eagles, only the crowned eagle is not yet endangered, probably because it lives in forests all over Africa.**

● **The harpy eagle of Central and South America is the largest eagle in the world. This huge predator is over 3 ft. (1 m) tall with thick, powerful legs and feet.**

Breeding

Although forest eagles hunt below the canopy, their courtship flights take them high above it. They call loudly as they soar to warn other eagles that the territory, often more than 135 square miles (350 km²) in extent, is theirs alone to hunt and mate within. This long-distance advertising is a good way of avoiding fights; for birds as powerfully armed as eagles, fighting can be lethal.

Crowned eagles mate for life. However, when one partner dies, the survivor finds a new mate. One nest that was watched for

A young crowned eagle soars over the African forest canopy. Soon it will be time for it to find a breeding territory of its own.

A female crowned eagle has laid two eggs. Unless there is plenty of food during the season, only one of the eaglets will survive.

second always dies, either from starvation because it cannot compete for food with the older chick or from the older chick killing it. This might seem wasteful, but it is presumably an insurance policy in case something goes wrong with the first egg.

Both the crowned eagle and the harpy eagle can breed only every other year. This is because they feed their young for nearly a year after it has flown from the nest, leaving them no time to rear another chick until the first can hunt its own food. If the surviving young bird dies, the parents will usually breed again within six months. The Philippine eagle probably does the same, but no one knows for sure.

20 years was used by three females and two males. The members of the pair changed, but they used the same nest for all that time. This is usual among large eagles, probably because their nests are so big that there would not be time to build a new one each season. The pair simply adds a few new sticks, often with green leaves on them.

The male crowned eagle brings food for his partner while they repair the nest and mate. With so little difference between the seasons in the rain forest, birds can breed at almost any time of year.

Large eagles sometimes lay two eggs, but only one of the eaglets grows up; the

Deadly Hunters

All three forest eagles are powerful hunters; their short toes are armed with sharp talons on rather thick,

The Butcher

IN FOCUS

One crowned eagle was observed as it caught a half-grown bushbuck, a species of forest antelope, twice its own weight. The bird butchered it before feeding. It removed the bushbuck's legs and head, wedging them in trees for eating later, then tore the body in two and dragged the pieces nearly 50 ft. (15 m) through the bush, where it finally ate them.

strong legs. They hit their prey hard and kill it by the sheer force of their grip when their talons pierce a vital organ.

The harpy eagle is a spectacular hunter. More than 3 feet (1 m) from head to tail and weighing nearly 11 pounds (5 kg), it flies among the tall trees, feeding mainly on macaws (muh-KAWS), large parrots of nearly the same length but nothing like the same weight. It also eats monkeys and three-toed sloths, which weigh up to 10 pounds (4.5 kg), only a little less than the eagle. Sloths hang underneath branches while they feed; the eagle swoops in and rolls over at the last moment, reaching

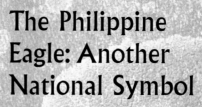

The Philippine Eagle: Another National Symbol

The Philippine eagle, the national bird of those islands, was originally called the monkey-eating eagle; its English name was changed in the 1980s for reasons of national dignity. Its scientific name is still pithecophagus, which means "monkey-eater."

The Philippine eagle is the second largest in the world. Here, it has caught a guinea pig, or cavy, unusually small prey for this huge bird.

upward to snatch the sloth from its branch. The Philippine eagle hunts no less dramatically than the harpy, grabbing monkeys out of trees as it flies by.

Crowned eagles feed mainly on mammals that they kill on the ground, often by dropping on them from a tree as the prey walks underneath. Their most common prey are hyraxes (small mammals common in rocky parts of the savanna) and young antelope, though they also eat large reptiles. Crowned eagles eat monkeys only where they are the most numerous prey animals. African monkeys are too observant and agile to be caught easily; eagles prefer food that is less accomplished at escaping.

One female can eat over one pound (500 g) of Suni antelope meat at one meal, but a pair that catches a vervet monkey weighing nearly 6 pounds (2.6 kg) will often make it last for more than a week between them, eating only about 3.5 ounces (100 g) per meal. It seems that although forest eagles need large territories to find food while they are feeding young, they can manage on a surprisingly small amount of food at other times of the year.

The harpy eagle can catch sloths from the trees where they hang and carry them away, though they weigh nearly as much as the eagle itself.

Deforestation in the Philippines has put the Philippine eagle in great danger, and damage to the forests of South America has made the harpy eagle rare. Only the crowned eagle seems to be doing well.

One serious problem for all the great eagles is their slow breeding rate. If a female lives for 13 years, of which she spends 10 years breeding, she will produce at most five young. It is highly unlikely that they will all survive. In fact a typical female leaves behind only one or two surviving offspring when she dies. For a population under pressure, this is not a high enough rate of replacement.

Unlike many other forest animals, the great eagles are not guaranteed to be saved by setting aside reserves for them because they need such huge territories. It may already be too late to save the one hundred or so Philippine eagles that may still survive: they continue to be hunted as trophies. As for the harpy, large areas of the Amazon forests have not yet been cleared, leaving them room to hunt, though time is running out.

Threats and Conservation

Forest eagles are not persecuted by farmers for stealing their livestock as eagles are in other parts of the world, mainly because the farmers rarely see them. By the time the rain forest has been turned into farmland, the eagles have long since disappeared. As with most other rain forest animals, the main threat to rain forest eagles is the loss of their habitat.

Check these out:
● Bird ● Canopy ● Endangered Species
● Food Web ● Human Interference

Ecology is the study of how living things interact with one another and with their environment. The high canopy of branches, the understory of smaller trees and shrubs, and the forest floor all provide different living conditions and have their own particular communities of plants and animals. There are complex chains of eating and being eaten, of hunting and being hunted. Animal droppings fertilize the soil, while plants take nutrients out of it. In turn, many animals eat the plants, absorbing and using the nutrients for energy. All these cycles are connected and contribute to the ecology of rain forests.

KEY FACTS

● Antbirds and other insect-eating birds follow army ant columns, snapping up insects that fly up to flee from the ants.

● Some species of forest frogs, lizards, and squirrels have evolved membranes of skin that allow them to glide through the air from tree to tree.

● Leaf-cutter ants carry leaves and blossoms into their underground nests, where they cultivate fungi that the ants then eat.

Competing Plants

Plants affect the climate within the forest. The trees keep out the wind and also give off moisture, making the air inside the forest very humid. The warm, moist conditions lead to high rates of plant growth. The plants compete for light, food, and space.

Under the forest canopy, a lot of light is absorbed by the foliage above. Plants of the forest floor survive because they can cope with low levels of light. Some have large leaves to absorb more light or colored leaves to exploit the particular colors of light that penetrate deep shade.

Almost every plant surface is home to another plant or fungus. Mosses grow on leaves; ferns, orchids, and bromeliads (broe-MEE-lee-ads) grow on high branches; and fungi (FUN-jie) grow on and in living and dead logs.

Depending on Each Other

For many forest plants, animals are important for carrying pollen from one plant to another and for dispersing their seeds and fruits. The dense vegetation makes it hard for pollen grains

Dead leaves rot down, releasing nutrients into soil. These feed plants, which produce nectar to feed insects, which are eaten by frogs.

IN FOCUS

Specialists

It is better for a flower if its pollinators are specialists; if the insects feed only on one species, all the pollen they pick up is likely to be carried to a flower of the right kind. So plants make their flowers attractive to one particular kind of insect and less attractive to others. For example, flowers pollinated by long-tongued insects or birds have narrow, tubular flowers that other insects cannot climb into. This has advantages for the insects, too, as they meet less competition for the nectar.

to travel on the wind, so transportation by insects, birds, and bats is more reliable. The animals rely on plants for food in the form of pollen, nectar, fruits, and nuts. As they feed, they carry pollen to other flowers and pass out seeds with their droppings.

High rates of plant growth and a huge variety of plant species support a wide range of animal species. Plants offer shelters and homes—places to build nests, places to dig out burrows under roots, and places to hide from predators. Leaves and twigs provide nesting material and bedding for birds, badgers, mice, and even chimpanzees and gorillas.

The droppings of animals and the dead remains of animals and plants—fallen leaves and flowers, dead twigs, and fallen trees—collect on the forest floor and rot, returning nutrients to the soil for plants to use again. The breakdown of this material involves many microscopic soil animals, bacteria, and fungi, as well as larger animals such as ants, termites, wood-boring beetles, and, in some forests, land crabs.

Adapting to the Environment

In a tropical rain forest there are no marked seasons like those found in the temperate zone, although some have both rainy and dry periods. Plants of the same species may be in flower or fruit all year round. This makes it possible for some animals to be specialists: bats that eat only fruit, sloths that feed on just a few species of trees. Some animals, such as the tiny honey possum of Australian forests, feed exclusively on nectar.

Certain animal characteristics suit their environment. Animals such as the sifaka (suh-FA-kuh) and orangutan have evolved long arms to swing from branch to branch, while spider monkeys have prehensile tails that act like fifth hands for curling around branches. Forest eagles and falcons have shorter wings to avoid getting tangled in the branches and long tails for precise steering in the canopy. Tree frogs have suction pads on their feet for clinging upside down on leaves. Rain forest plants and animals have evolved such an intricate web of relationships that most species cannot survive anywhere else.

Check these out:
- Carnivore ● Ecosystem ● Evolution of the Rain Forest ● Food Web ● Herbivore ● Insectivore ● Rain Forest

An ecosystem is made up of a community of living organisms and the nonliving parts of their surroundings. Living organisms include plants, animals, fungi (FUN-jie), and bacteria. Water, soil, sunlight, and air make up the nonliving part of the ecosystem. In a rain forest ecosystem, the number of different species of plants, animals, and fungi—its biodiversity—is enormous. Nobody can say how many there are, but it seems likely that all together, tropical rain forests may contain over 30 million different species. Many thousands of these are insects.

Rain falls all through the year, with only a brief dry season. Indeed, rain may still fall then, although not as much as at other times of the year. The amount of rain generally ranges between 95 and 155 inches (2,500 mm to 4,000 mm) a year, although some of the wettest forests receive up to 360 inches (9,000 mm). Tropical rain forests are always warm, and there are no winters. The abundance of water and warmth means that plants grow quickly and in great profusion.

Some patches of rain forest have been in continuous existence since the Pleistocene epoch, around 2 million years ago. This combination of age, warmth, and ample rainfall makes the tropical rain forest

KEY FACTS

● A rain forest provides many different kinds of habitats where animals can live and find food.

● Tropical rain forests may contain over 30 million different species of animals and plants, most of which are not yet named or described.

The vegetation bordering a rain forest river is particularly dense because of the extra light that enters through the gap created by open water.

ecosystem different from all other forests. Only these forests provide the climate and conditions suitable for the survival of such a tremendous diversity of plant and animal species. Temperate rain forests are evergreen but do not support the vast biodiversity found in tropical rain forests.

Habitats

The crowns of rain forest trees make a continuous green canopy high above the ground. Scattered throughout these are even taller trees, called emergents, with crowns that overtop the canopy. Scrambling climbers, or lianas (lee-AH-nuhs), link the trees. The complex structure of a rain forest, with its leafy canopy, towering emergents, climbers, patches of dense undergrowth, shady forest floor, and brightly lit riverbanks, provides a mosaic of many different habitats where different animals can live and find food.

Competition

Although the luxurious vegetation provides food and living space for many different kinds of animals, competition for space, light, and food is still intense. Young trees must wait for an old tree to fall before the sunlight can reach them and they can grow. The leaves of climbers compete with the foliage of the trees supporting their twining stems.

Different kinds of animals compete for and occupy every part of the rain forest. The particular habitat of each species and the way that it uses the resources in its habitat is called its niche. For example, although three different kinds of fruit- and leaf-eating colobus monkeys live in the canopy of western African rain forests, each occupies a different niche. The red colobus roves among the highest branches;

the black-and-white colobus lives in the middle of the canopy; and the olive colobus dwells among the lower branches.

Other kinds of animals, such as tapirs and peccaries, occupy niches on the forest floor. Some kinds, such as crowned eagles, live or fly high in the tops of the tallest trees. Many, including iguanas, coatis (mammals related to raccoons), and chimpanzees, are more versatile, foraging on the floor and up among the lianas and boughs of the canopy. Some are nocturnal, waking up only at night, and others are active by day. Using different niches at different times of day or night helps avoid competition for food and space.

IN FOCUS

Keystone Species

Fruit is an important part of the diet of many forest animals, especially many of those living in the leafy canopy. Although there are no winters or long dry spells, many forest trees bear fruit only once or twice a year. This means there are times when fruit is scarce. Some, such as figs, bear fruit all year. Because they are so valuable in these otherwise fruitless intervals, they are known as keystone species.

Sunshine

The sun gives warmth and light. Plants need sunlight for photosynthesis and arrange their leaves so that the sun can fall on them. Plants can grow extremely quickly wherever there is enough light.

Fragile Forest

The rain forest ecosystem is the sum of all its parts. If the system is disrupted or parts are removed, it will collapse. When large areas are logged, habitats are lost and so are animals and decomposers. The soil washes away. If animals are driven to extinction, then the plants that they pollinate cannot set fruit and reproduce.

Clearings

When a forest giant dies and falls, it tears a large hole in the canopy. Sunlight floods the gap down to the ground, enabling seedlings to germinate and saplings to shoot upward.

Decomposers

Dead animals, droppings, old leaves, branches, flowers, uneaten fruit, and eventually entire trees fall to the forest floor. There, in the permanently moist environment, fungi and bacteria swiftly break down anything not eaten by a passing scavenger. These decomposers are vital to the functioning of the ecosystem.

Nutrient Recycling

The decomposer uses some of the nutrients released during decomposition, but the rest are released into the air as gases or remain in the top layer of soil, ready to be absorbed by living plants. The decomposers work at a rapid rate, enabling a quick turnover of nutrients such as phosphates and potassium.

Herbivores

Herbivorous animals, those that eat only plants, are called primary consumers. All parts of the forest's plants are eaten by something. Sloths feed on foliage, fruit bats eat fruit, longhorn beetle larvae (grubs) eat wood, and marmosets feed on gummy tree sap.

Animals

Rain forests teem with many different kinds of mammals, birds, reptiles, amphibians, and invertebrates, and their rivers are full of freshwater fish. People also live in the rain forests. People and other animals depend on the rain forest plants.

Leafy canopy
Although a true rain forest always has a leafy green canopy, within it individual trees may be completely leafless for brief periods. Rain forest trees often flower after they have shed their leaves.

Rainfall
Water evaporates from the leaves quickly in the hot sun, but the high rainfall in the rain forest prevents them from wilting and shriveling. It allows epiphytes to survive perched on branches high in the canopy, their roots absorbing rain as it trickles past.

Plants
Using photosynthesis, plants can make simple sugars—the starting point for all the other substances that make up the plant. Because of this, plants are known as producers: they produce food for animals to eat. All the other living organisms in the rain forest ecosystem are dependent on them.

IN FOCUS

Rain Forest Soil

The tall rain forest trees grow on soils that are often shallow, frequently acidic, and poor in nutrients. These nutrients, especially nitrates, are concentrated near the surface, where fallen leaves and other debris speedily decay. To take advantage of this, most of the roots of trees and other plants grow in just the top 12 in. (30 cm) of soil, forming a spreading mat.

Predators
Plant–eating herbivores are eaten by predators. These carnivorous animals are known as secondary consumers. Larger predators will catch and eat them. In fact many rain forest animals are omnivores that eat a wide range of different kinds of plants and animals.

Check these out:
- Canopy ● Carnivore
- Climate and Weather ● Ecology
- Food Web ● Forest Floor ● Herbivore
- Insectivore ● Rain Forest ● Season

Eels swim in rivers and swamps throughout the world's tropical rain forests. Usually nocturnal and often highly secretive, they lurk in mud and dense aquatic vegetation, lying in wait for their prey. Almost all feed mainly on other fish but will also eat frogs and aquatic invertebrates.

Eels can travel great distances across land, often up to 550 yards (500 m). Many can gulp air to keep themselves well supplied with oxygen, provided their gills are kept moist. As they usually travel in this way at night after heavy rain, keeping their skin moist is not a problem. They produce large quantities of mucus that also prevents them from drying out.

Swamp Eels

Swamp eels are found in the swampy rain forests of western Africa and Malaysia. They collect in the deepest parts of the swamp when the dry season begins, to avoid being left high and dry. Swamp eels dig holes in the soft, submerged mud and sit with their heads sticking out.

In Central America swamp eels grow to about 27 inches (70 cm) in length. They inhabit the rivers but during the wet season migrate into swamps and temporary pools. As the wet season draws to a close and their pools dry up, they often have to cross the forest floor to return to the river. Muddy swamps have a poor oxygen content, so the swamp eels surface to swallow air.

The fire eel lives in rivers throughout Indonesia. It is very popular for aquariums.

Electric eels

The electric eel is found in rivers in the northern part of South America. An electric eel can grow to 8 feet (2.5 m) long and weigh almost 110 pounds (50 kg). It can stun or kill its prey by producing a jolt of electricity of up to five hundred volts, generating this electricity in electroplates within its tail. This jolt of electricity is also used as a form of protection. Even horses have been brought down as they have waded through shallow rivers.

The rain forest rivers of India, Sri Lanka, and Indonesia are inhabited by smaller eels such as spiny and fire eels. These grow up to 16 inches (40 cm) in length. They normally possess two small tentacles on their snout, which they use to detect prey. They too are nocturnal and feed on worms and fish.

Check these out:
● Fish   ● Flooding   ● Nocturnal Animal   ● Water

A small group of Asian elephants feeds in the depths of a forest. Very little of their natural habitat remains.

Elephants are the largest living land mammals. They appear to have evolved so large in order to exploit the very poor plant material that is available to them. To digest such poor food, an animal needs a large stomach.

Elephants are vegetarian browsers, picking off the youngest leaves of trees and shrubs. The elephant's trunk is an essential part of feeding, used for sniffing out tender leaves and nipping them off. It is also used for drinking.

There are two species of elephant—the African elephant and the Asian elephant.

Asian Elephants

The Asian elephant lives in parts of India, Sri Lanka, Indonesia, Malaysia, and China, though it is endangered. It is the smaller of the two elephant species, yet its vital statistics are still impressive. Known to live for around 60 years, it stands at around 8 feet (2.5 m) at the shoulder, and an adult bull can weigh around 11,000 pounds (5,000 kg). Asian elephants are so large that they simply force their way through the dense forest undergrowth. In this way they provide other rain forest animals with open tracks to follow.

Cow and bull elephants live separately. The females live in family groups of mothers, sisters, and daughters. If a bull is born, he will stay in this female group until he is old enough to join a bachelor herd.

African Rain Forest Elephants

Although the African elephant is a plains and open woodland species, there is one subspecies that inhabits the rain forests of the Democratic Republic of the Congo and western Africa. African rain forest elephants are now rare, and little is known of their behavior. The only time they are on full view is when they emerge from the forest to feed in open swampland or bathe in the river. They play a vital role in keeping some of these forest clearings open for other animals.

Check these out:

● Endangered Species ● Herbivore ● Mammal

Emergents are tall trees that stick out, or emerge, from the general canopy of the rain forest. Their branches open out like giant umbrellas way above the rest of the trees. They include some of the world's tallest trees, although they rarely rival the giant redwoods of North America or the enormous eucalyptus trees in the cooler parts of Australia.

Emergent trees are most common in lowland tropical forests. Upland areas get more wind and the giant trees would probably be blown over. The tallest emergent trees in the tropical rain forests are the klinki pines that grow in the forests of New Guinea. These cone-bearing trees, closely related to the monkey puzzle tree, can reach heights of over 295 feet (90 m).

IN FOCUS

Buttress Roots

Towering above the rest of the forest, emergent trees are always being buffeted by the wind; they need extra-strong root systems to stop them from being blown over. Most of them develop buttress roots, which are like wooden walls spreading out from the bases of the trunks. They take the strain when the trees are rocked by the wind. The buttress roots of ceiba may extend 33 ft. (10 m) or more up its trunk.

Emergent trees are usually scattered around the rain forest, but in some areas they grow quite close together and form an additional canopy or roof, a sort of forest above a forest. The klinki pines of New Guinea, for example, form a high roof as much as 195 feet (60 m) above the rest of the trees. Huge trees of this kind are sometimes known as superemergents.

Brazil nut trees grow to about 195 feet (60 m) in the South American rain forests, and a member of the pea family known as *Dinizia excelsa* reaches 215 feet (65 m). The ceiba (SAE-buh) tree—also known as the kapok or silk cotton tree—sometimes reaches 230 feet (70 m). These trees grow in the African rain forests as well as in South America. They are the tallest trees in Africa. Big buttress roots support their massive trunks.

A clump of dipterocarp trees towers high above the tangled vegetation springing up in a clearing of lowland rain forest in Southeast Asia.

Other African emergents include the African mahogany, also called sapele, and the African teak, or iroko. Both of these are important timber trees. The African teak is especially valuable because it is not attacked by termites.

The rain forests of Southeast Asia contain more emergent species than the other rain forests. The largest are the huge klinki pines already mentioned, but they are closely followed by tualang trees of the pea family. These trees grow in Malaysia and have been known to reach a height of 275 feet (84 m). They are the tallest known flowering trees in the Tropics. The most common emergent trees in Southeast Asia belong to a large group known as dipterocarps. Named for their two-winged seeds, these trees reach heights of about 165 feet (50 m). They often grow close together, especially in the slightly drier areas of the forest. Their leaves are often yellowish green, and from the air their crowns look like clusters of giant cauliflowers. The dipterocarps provide a lot of valuable timber.

Ceiba timber is used for plywood, but the tree is best known for the silky fibers that surround its seeds, which are used for stuffing sleeping bags and life jackets. Ceiba trees are cultivated in huge plantations in Africa and Southeast Asia.

Because the emergent trees are so big, they are sought after for the timber trade. They are often the first to disappear from the rain forests, and many other trees are destroyed in the process of felling and removing the giants.

Check these out:
● Light Gap ● Logging ● Rain Forest ● Tree

Glossary

Bacteria: a tiny organism, one of the smallest forms of life, that may be made up of a single cell or many cells.

Biodiversity: the total number of different kinds of living organisms in an area or ecosystem.

Biome: a large area that is distinguished by its climate and vegetation. Tropical rain forest is one type of biome, desert is another kind of biome.

Bromeliad: any of over one thousand plants of the pineapple family with a crown of stiff, spiny leaves. Some bromeliads grow on the ground, but most of them perch on trees.

Cellulose: a white chemical substance that forms the walls of plant cells and gives shape to the plant.

Condensation: water produced by mist or steam when it cools.

Ecosystem: a group of plants and animals that interact with each other in an area (called their environment). A single tree and a whole forest are both ecosystems.

Electroplate: that part of an eel's electric organ that produces the electricity, made of a thin sheet of muscle. There are around five thousand electroplates in each electric organ.

Endemic: a disease that is native to the area where it is found.

Enzyme: a substance that assists in chemical changes without itself being used up in the process.

Epiphyte: a name given to any plant that grows on another without taking any food from it. Most epiphytes grow on trees.

Ethnobotanist: a person who studies the traditional uses of plants by native tribes, usually for medecine, sometimes for food or clothing.

Germinate: when seeds sprout and start to grow.

Head-hunting: the practise of removing the heads of enemies as trophies of warfare.

Hydroelectricity: electricity generated by the power of falling water.

Indigenous: plants, animals, or people that are local to an area.

Infectious: a disease that is passed from person to person in water supplies, by insect or other animal, or by physical contact.

Invertebrate: an animal that does not possess a backbone or vertebra, for example an insect or worm.

Latitude: the distance, measuring north and south, of a place from the equator, which is at 0° latitude.

Niche: the range of habitat conditions and resources in which a particular species is able to live.

Parasite: an animal that lives off other animals of different species, and which often has a harmful effect on its host.

Photosynthesis: the process by which green plants use the energy in sunlight to make sugar from carbon dioxide and water.

Plywood: board made by gluing several thin sheets of timber together in such a way that the grain of one sheet runs at right angles to the grain of the next sheet. This gives the board extra strength.

Regurgitate: the process of coughing up food either to rechew it or to feed it to offspring.

Rut: the mating season for deer, when males fight to establish the right to mate with the females.

Index

Numbers in *italics* indicate
    photographs.

Africa 114, 124–125, 129, 141, 146
Aka people 129
Amazon 115, 128, 146
anoles 122
ants 121, 123, 163
    leaf-cutter 162
Asia 114
Australia 115

baboons 123
bacteria 140–141, 151, 163–164
Baka people 125
beetles 141, 163
    carrion 141
    dung 141
Belize 129
biodiversity 164–165
birds: communication 121–123
    courtship 132
    species of:
        antbirds 162
        argus pheasant 122
        birds of paradise 132
        bowerbirds 132
        cassowaries 122
        cocks-of-the-rock 132
        curassows 133
        eagles 158–161, 163
            crowned 158–161,
                158–159, 165
            harpy 158–161, *161*
            Philippine, or monkey-
                eating 158–161, *160*
        flycatchers 125
        gray parrots 125
        hornbills 125
        pigeons 133
        toucans 123
        vultures 141
Bolivia 146
Borneo 156–157
Brazil 146–147, 151
bromeliads 120, 139, 155, 162
bush meat 125
butterflies 123
buttress roots 170, *170*

caimans 134–137
    black 137
    dwarf, or smooth-fronted
        135, 137
    spectacled *134*, 136

camouflage 131
canopy 116–117, 124, 129, 153,
    165, 167, 170–171
carbon dioxide 115, 148
carnivores 167
caterpillars 121
cats 123, 133
cattle ranching 147
cellulose 140
Central African Republic 129
chimpanzees 125, 129, 165
cicadas 121–122, 133
climate, forest 114–115, 124,
    162, 164–165
climate, world 115
climbers 116–117, 165
coatis 165
cobras, king 118–119, *118–119*
cockroaches:
    giant tropical
        cockroaches 120
    hissing cockroaches 120, *120*
    wood roaches 120
Colombia 146
communication 121–123
Congo 124–125
conservation 126–129, 141
copepods 138, *138*
Costa Rica 129
courtship 132–133
crabs 138–139, 141, 163
    Caribbean land 139
    coconut 138
    hermit 138
    red land *139*
crickets 121–122, *121*
crocodiles 134–137
    Johnston's, or freshwater
        135, 136
    mugger, or marsh 135, *137*
    New Guinea 135, *135*
    saltwater or estuarine
        135, *135*
    West African dwarf 135
crustaceans 138–139
    crabs (See CRABS)
    shrimps 138
    wood lice 138–139

dam building 147–148, 151–152
decomposers 140–141, 166
deer 123, 142–145
    axis, or chital 143, *143*

muntjac 142, 145, *145*
red brocket 144–145, *144*
sambar *142*, 145
Visayan spotted 145
deforestation 125, 146–149, 171
diseases 150–151
    malaria 150–151
    onchocerciasis or river
        blindness 150–151
    Schistosomiasis, or
        bilharziasis 150–151
    yellow fever 150–151
dolphins
    botos 152, *152*
    susus 152
dormancy 153
dragonflies and damselflies
        154–155
    aeshnid 154
    giant damselfly 155, *155*
Dyak people 156–157

ecological niche 165
ecology 162–163
Ecuador 146
eels
    electric 168
    fire 168, *168*
    spiny 168
    swamp 168
Efe people 125
elephants
    African 125, 129, 169
    Asian, 169, *169*
emergent 165, 170–171
endangered species 126–129,
        135–136, 145, 161
epiphytes 117, 120
ethnobotanists 157
extinction 146–148

farming 125, 128–129, 147–148
ferns 162
figs 165, *165*
fireflies 133
fish 123
flowers
    African violets 124
    white arum lilies 124
flies 141
forest floor 165
frogs 121, 132–133, 163

red-eyed leaf frogs *132*
fruit 117
fungi 140–141, *141,* 162–164

galagos 123
gibbons *117*
global warming 115, 148
gorillas 124–125, 129
   eastern lowland 125, *125*
grasshoppers 122

herbivores 166–167
honey possums 163
humidity 114–115, 162
hunter-gatherers 125, 129

Iban people 156
iguanas 165
indris 147
Ivory Coast 146

keystone species 165

leopards 133
lianas 116–117, 121, 165
light gaps 153
lizards *122,* 123, 141
logging 125, 129, 147, 149, 157

Madagascar 146–147
Malaysia *147*
Mbuti people 125, 149
medicinal plants 148, 151, 157
   quinine 151
Mexico 146
millipedes 140, 141
   giant pill *140*
mining 129, 148, 151–152
monkeys 116, 121–123, 133
   colobus 165
   Howler 123, *123*
   langur 143, *143*
monsoon 114
mosquitoes 121, 122,
   150–151, *150*

national parks 125–126,
   128–129
   Dzanga-Ndoki National
      Park 129
   Kahuzi-Biega National
      Park 125

naturalists 127–128
nectar 116
nest-building 163
Nigeria 146
nocturnal animals 120, 130, 140

okapis 125
orangutans 163
orchids 162

palm, climbing 116–117
parasites 150–151
peccaries 165
Philippines 146
photosynthesis 115
plantation, tree 128, 147, 171
poaching 128
pollination 128, 162–163
pollution 152
praying mantis 133, *133*

rainfall 114–115, *115,* 124,
   164, 167
rattans 117
reptiles 118–119, 134–137
rivers 130, 152
road building 129, 148

shade toleration 162
sifakas 163
slash-and-burn cultivation 147
sloths 163
snakes: camouflage 131
   constrictors 130–131
   nesting 119
   species of:
      anaconda 130
      boa 130–131
         rainbow *130,* 131
      gaboon vipers 125
      king cobra 118–119,
        118–119
      kraits 119
      pythons 119, 130–131
         green tree 131, *131*
         Indian 130
         ringed 131
      rat snakes 119
      venom 118–119
soil 148, 167
Southeast Asia 146, 148
spiders 122

strangler figs 117
Swiss cheese plants 117

tapirs 165
temperate rain forest
   114–115, 165
temperature 114–115
termites 140, 163
Thailand 146
tigers 133
tortoises 141
tourism 128–129, 137
trees: hardwoods 124–125, 128,
   146, 148–149
   softwoods 147
   species of:
      brazil nut 170
      ceiba (capok or silk
        cotton) 170–171
      Dinizia excelsa 170
      dipterocarp 171, *171*
      ebony 124, 146
      iroko (African teak) 125,
        146, 171
      klinki pines 170–171
      oil palm 124
      rubber 147
      sapele (African
        mahogany) 124,
        146, 171
      Sitka spruce 153
      teak 146–147, 171
      tualang 171
tree shrews 123, 133
Twa people 125

United Nations Environment
   Programme 127
United States 115

water 114–115
World Conservation Monitoring
   Center 127
World Conservation Union
   (IUCN) 127
Worldwide Fund for Nature
   (WWF) 127, 129
worms 140, 151

Yanomami people 149, 151